MADE FOR JOY

A Study on Conversion & Prayer

Parish Life Services Press
850 Watershed Dr.
Ann Arbor, MI 48105
www.ParishLifeServices.org
ISBN:1-929148-57-7

Printed in the United States of America

Embracing God's Plan for Our Life

PART I: CONVERSION & PRAYER

(Part II: Ongoing Conversion, begins on page 61)

Introduction

IS CHRISTIANITY IRRELEVANT?

A conversation between two seminary professors in a P.D. James mystery novel raises the question of Christianity's relevance today. Both profs are resident at a seminary during the murder of its most senior official and remain suspects. The conversation takes a surprising turn over the question of whether their colleagues really have faith:

> [George] "Oh they believe, all right. Its just that what they believe has become irrelevant. I don't mean the moral teaching: the Judeo-Christian heritage has created Western civilization and we should be grateful to it. But the church they serve is dying. When I look at the *Doom* [a masterpiece painting owned by the seminary] I try to have some understanding of what it meant to 15th-century men and women. If life is hard and short and full of pain you need the hope of heaven; if there is no effective law, you need the deterrent of law. The church gave them comfort and light and pictures and stories and the hope of everlasting life. The 21st century has other compensations. Football for one. There you have ritual, color, drama, the sense of belonging; football has its high priests, even its martyrs. And then there's shopping, art, music, travel, alcohol, drugs. We all have our own resources for staving off those two horrors of human life, boredom and the knowledge that we die. And now – God help us – there's the Internet. Pornography at the touch of a few keys. If you want to find a pedophile ring or discover how to make a bomb to blow up people you disagree with, it's all there for you. Plus, of course, a bottomless mine of other information. Some of it even accurate."
>
> Emma said, "But when all these things fail, even the music, the poetry, the art?"
>
> [George] "Then my dear, I shall turn to science. If my end promises to be unpleasant, I shall rely on morphine, and the compassion of my doctor. Or perhaps I shall swim out to sea and take my last look at the sky."[a]

Is George correct about Christianity? Is its moral teaching the only enduring value of this ancient religion?

---

[a] page 281, *Death in Holy Orders*, P.D. James, NY: Ballantine, 2001

OR IS CHRISTIANITY THE SOURCE OF TRUE JOY?

Perhaps a certain medieval appeal of Christianity has melted away as resources, freedom, leisure and art have grown plentiful. Yet what about the deeper human longing for joy? Does Christianity hold the key to our happiness and joy?

Are you looking for joy, true joy? Not simply the flush of success or a wave of pleasure. Nor the passing elation of achievement, the fleetingness of sensible delight, or a temporary abatement from the stresses of life. All of us look for true joy unless, in frustration, we deny its existence. In fact, God knows each of us, loves us deeply, and made us to experience joy and even *longs* for us to embrace it. The fundamental source of this joy is knowing God and enjoying his love for us through Jesus Christ.

So why isn't everyone aglow with joy? Don't most people claim to be Christians? The answer is that a relationship with God depends upon embracing his plan for our lives, beginning with asking for God's forgiveness and to be in a relationship with Him and surrendering our life completely to God. We must "do what he tells us" which translates to not only concrete changes in our lives but a radical re-working of our whole life and identity. God's plan has several key elements that are common to everyone:

1. Being with God and His people;
2. Becoming like Jesus; and
3. Loving whom God loves.

Each of these elements is ultimately a source of indescribable joy. Being with the incredible wellspring of all beauty, goodness, and truth, who is the most fascinating and engaging of persons, who himself has a deep and tender love for each of us will make us very happy. Becoming like Jesus aligns us with the deep identity that God calls us to: being a person of love, joy, peace, and goodness *made capable* of deep relationships with God and his people. Relationships with God and people who are like him is simply where joy comes from. This joy overflows and is amplified as we express our love and care for those around us. True and eternal joy only comes from embracing his plan for us. All other joys are but faint glimmers of such bliss.

As God is the master-builder of our lives, he not only has the plan but, upon our request, does most of the work! This study considers God's promise of the eternal joy of being with him and his people through his power at work within us. This brief book describes only the general characteristics of God's plan rather than all the details of building, or, perhaps, of remodeling, our lives except for its overall focus on prayer[a]. Indeed, prayer – simply being with God and asking for his help – is one of the necessary requirements for God working in our life.

---

[a] *Made for Joy* is the introduction to a series of titles devoted to Catholic spiritual formation and discipleship, *Embracing God's Plan for Your Life.*

Although this study is suitable for any time of year, the spiritual sobriety of Lent is particularly fitting. Indeed, many good things and the quest for many more good things fill our life, ranging from a nice house to fascinating amusements. As one spiritual writer notes, the good is often the enemy of the best[a]. The sobriety with which Catholics meet Lent – setting aside good things for the sake of pursuing the best – also helps us focus on God's overall plan for our lives. Only when we cease drinking cola can our palates adjust to champagne; only when we rest our appetites from pizza can we appreciate lobster. In Lent, we fast from some good earthly pleasures in order to feast more on God himself through prayer.

Turning our gaze from earthly pleasures frees us to see the joy God intends for us. Regardless of when you begin this study, try to quiet your appetites for the good things of this world better to consider the riches of eternal life with God.

How lovely is your dwelling place,
O LORD of hosts!
My soul longs, indeed it faints for the courts of the LORD;
my heart and my flesh sing for joy to the living God (Ps 84.1-2)

Entering into the Very Life of God

Grace is a *participation in the life of God.* It introduces us into the intimacy of Trinitarian life: by Baptism the Christian participates in the grace of Christ, the Head of his Body. As an "adopted son" he can henceforth call God "Father," in union with the only Son. He receives the life of the Spirit who breathes charity into him and who forms the Church . . . Spiritual progress tends toward ever more intimate union with Christ.

Catechism of the Catholic Church (hereafter "CCC"), 1997, 2014

---

[a] Dawson Trottman writing in the middle of the last century.
[e] See CCC 1026.

4

1 - Being with God: Our Joy and Our Delight

AN EMBARRASSMENT OF JOY

In your presence there is fullness of joy.

Psalm 16.11

I was rather embarrassed over this smile I couldn't wipe off my face. I looked away from the clerk on my way to find some ointment for my cracked lips. It was too weird. I worried about the cashier thinking I was on drugs. "But why cover my face? What am I embarrassed about?" I remembered tasting joy before, like opening Christmas presents at grandma's house, but this was a deeper joy. It had an effervescent quality. Believe me, I wasn't complaining. In fact, it made me think of a fabled pleasure machine my freshmen philosophy prof had described recently – who would disengage once hooked up? Only my endless smile reflected a newfound awareness of God's presence and love for me rather than sensual pleasure.

A few days earlier, I left the library to stretch my legs. When studying my smile retired into a sort of Mona Lisa look of bemusement. My heart filled with gratitude and joy, while circling the block, over a recent conversion on a retreat where we set aside our studies and worldly pursuits in order to seek after God and spend time with him.

GOD KNOWS AND LOVES *ME*?

I left that retreat with the conviction that God really *knew me*. What I expected logically about God's love for me from reading Scripture and from my Catholic upbringing somehow became very real. Indeed, *He is my father, He cares about me, He has counted every hair on my head*. If God is for me and loves me, what else really matters – what of all the things the people around me were pursuing: girls, grades, drink, song, being cool, and grad school? There was nothing sweeter than God's love, nothing sweeter than being in his presence.

God is a person (three, actually) rather than some far away abstraction and loves us with a personal love. I later found a passage from Scripture fitting this discovery:

> You shall be called My Delight Is in Her,
> and your land Married;
> for the Lord delights in you . . .
> as a bridegroom rejoices over the bride,
> so shall your God rejoice over you.
>
> Isaiah 62.4-5, NRSV

While I couldn't picture myself as a "bride", my youthful infatuations had taught me of unbridled delight in another person, which delight God took in me. *Why* God would delight in someone like me added mirth to my joy; best simply to enjoy the gift rather than question God's sanity!

We can't help but appreciate anyone who is merely fond of us. The intensity of God's absolute love can only provoke deep joy. Pure love leads to pure joy, a relation that defies analysis: it is simply a matter of how we are made. Of course, we can reject love, we can ignore it, put conditions on it, fail to trust it, and even deny its possibility as simply being too good to be true. Yet experiencing God's love but once is absolutely unforgettable. What a difference there is between a philosophical or even theological definition of love and the *experience* of God's love. Even though, as we shall see in chapters 4-6 on prayer, simply gazing or meditating upon God's great goodness, truth and beauty yields joy, God's personal love for us, his delight in us and him deeply desiring our company, is the heart of our joy.

Many people who continue to practice their faith as adults experience conversion as an adult; people's emotional experience of conversion varies a great deal, just as people's experience of God in prayer also varies. Most people, however, find joy in God's love for us and over how wonderful he is, especially while praying or worshiping, although the exact emotional character of such joy depends upon the individual. We do know that our life with God in heaven, where we will see him continuously and face to face, will be one of indescribable and glorious joy (I Peter 1.8). Access to God's presence, one way or another, depends upon the foundational work of Jesus[e], which we will consider in Chapters 2 and 3. This chapter considers God's promise of the greatest happiness from simply being with him.

WHAT ARE YOUR JOYS?

Let's first take some time to consider what gives you joy and makes you happy. What were your most enjoyable experiences of the last week?[a]

1. _____

---

[a] If you are coming off a rough week or are in a season of Lent where you happen to be fasting or abstaining from some of your favorite pleasures, think back to a more normal time to consider the joys of a typical week.

2.   _____

3.   _____

What were your most enjoyable experiences of the last year?

1.   _____

2.   _____

3.   _____

What's your greatest (day)dream? . . . starting in the NBA ? . . . having that perfect wedding? . . . gaining that elusive promotion? . . . grandchildren and a beach retirement?

_____

_____

_____

What makes these experiences so enjoyable? Try to answer that question (easier than it sounds) for one of your experiences.

_____

_____

_____

_____

As your reflections above probably bear out, we find delight in many ways. In fact, creation is good and is meant to delight us even as it delights God (See Genesis 1-2). Yet what is the best source of joy? The following criteria may help determine the best source of joy:

- How intense or fulfilling is the pleasure or joy?
- Does it last? Is it sustainable?
- Does it always "work"?
- Does it make you *deeply* happy?
- Does the experience get "old" with repetition?
- Does *too much* make you feel "bloated"?
- How dependable is the source of joy?

Indeed, many joys in our everyday life fulfill these criteria to some degree. But joys rooted in our natural life all lack in something; they make us long for something greater and more complete, for joy that utterly satisfies, lasts forever, never grows old or fades, and springs from an eternal and unchanging source. God is the only source of such joy, a joy fueled by his love for us and the wonder of his presence. Of course, since God himself is joyful, becoming like him and loving others as he does also fills us with joy, as does friendship with those similarly transformed into his likeness[a].

The second part of this chapter looks first at David's joy in God's presence and one way in which Jesus reveals his divinity and invites us into a relationship with himself filled with great joy. Indeed, just as David found God in his temple, we find God in Jesus.

JOY IN GOD'S TEMPLE

My Heart and Flesh Sing for Joy (Psalm 84.2)

King David exhibits a joy in God's presence that typifies Israel's ardor for God in the Old Testament :

> David again gathered all the chosen men of Israel, thirty thousand. David and all the people with him set out and went from Baale-judah, to bring up from there the ark of God, which is called by the name of the Lord of hosts who is enthroned on the cherubim. David and all the house of Israel were dancing before the Lord with all their might, with songs and lyres and harps and tambourines and castanets and cymbals. (2 Samuel 6:1-2,5; NRSV)

David's joy in parading the ark of God to Jerusalem is matched later by the exuberance of many psalms he authored or inspired. The ark of the covenant, or tabernacle, is also referred to as God's house or temple; the ark is soon to be the heart of Solomon's temple, its holy of holies. God had descended in glory upon the ark before Moses on Mt. Sinai, marking his presence by a column of fire at night and a cloud of smoke by day while leading the tribes of Israel into the promised land[c]. Transporting this supreme locus of God's presence[d] to Israel's new capital warranted tremendous celebration indeed.

The Book of Psalms, the prayer book and hymnal for temple worship in Jerusalem, reflects this same joy of being in God's presence. Consider some of the reasons found in the Psalms for David and his court rejoicing in God's presence[e] by completing the following table.

---

[a] See CCC 30; 1023-9, the latter of which describes Heaven and is my favorite passage in the entire Catechism.
[c] See Exodus 40.34-38; God also manifests his glorious presence upon completion of the Solomon's temple, see I Kings 8.10-13.
[d] CCC 2594.
[e] See the "For Further Study" section for some more background on the use of the Psalms in prayer.
[h] Many books of the New Testament employ temple imagery to describe God's presence.

<u>**Reason for Rejoicing**</u>

Ps26.7-8 _____

Ps 27.4 _____

Ps 43.3-4 _____

Ps 84.1-4,10 _____

Does King David have it right? Could it be that the source of true joy simply is being in God's presence? If so, how do we access God's presence since Jerusalem's temple was destroyed long ago? Can we be in his presence right now, every day, every hour?

Preserving Bible Times, Inc. "Reproduction of the City of Jerusalem at the time of the Second Temple"

JESUS, THE NEW TEMPLE

An Indescribable and Glorious Joy   I Peter 1.8

Jesus uses temple imagery as a starting point to speak about God's presence[h]. By Jesus' time, Solomon's temple had been built, destroyed, and rebuilt in tremendous majesty, but its days were numbered (the Romans would destroy it for good in another 40 years). Jesus declares himself greater than this great Temple (Matthew 12.6), one of the marvels of the ancient world. His Jewish audience, steeped in the Psalms and Temple worship, knew Jesus was claiming for himself a greater presence of God than the Temple held.

Indeed, the prologue of the Gospel of John uses a peculiar word in describing Jesus' time on earth – tabernacled – that alludes to the Temple:

> The Word [Jesus] became flesh and *tabernacled* among us, and we have seen his glory, the glory as of a father's only son, full of grace and truth[b].

Jesus was actually crucified in part for comparing himself to the Temple. Read Matthew 26.57-61 to find the convicting testimony. Why does Jesus' implicit claim to have power only belonging to God and being himself the place where God is most present anger the Jewish leaders? What further light does John 2.13-21 shed on this question?

_____

_____

_____

_____

The temple imagery reveals Jesus as the best "place" to find God (elsewhere in the Gospels Jesus lets us know, in fact, that he *is* the Son of God). We also see that Jesus explicitly describes himself as the *means* of gaining access to God's presence in the big windup discussion with his disciples the night before being arrested[c]:

Let not your hearts be troubled; believe in God, believe also in me. In my Father's house are many rooms; if it were not so, would I have told you that I go to prepare a place for you? And when I go and prepare a place for you, I will come again and will take you to myself, that where I am you may be also. And you know the way to the place where I am going. Thomas said to him, "Lord, we do not know where you are going. How can we know the way? Jesus said to him, "I am the way, and the truth, and the life. No one comes to the Father except through me. If you know me, you will know my Father also. From now on you do know him and have seen him." (John 14.1-7)

Jesus further invokes temple imagery to describe heaven as the "house of God", which is the literal interpretation of the Hebrew words for temple. Many psalms, for example, refer to the Temple as the house of God. In this passage Jesus quickly shifts from the temple imagery to more personal and intimate terms. Circle all the words in the following passage related to "seeing", "knowing" and "being together", "dwelling or abiding with one another":

---

[b] John 1.14. The Greek word translated here as "tabernacled" is translated as "lived among us" in the NRSV .
[c] See the Gospel of John, chapters 13-17, easily the longest continuous discourse in all of the gospels.

"If you love me, you will keep my commandments. And I will pray the Father, and he will give you another Counselor, to be with you for ever, even the Spirit of truth, whom the world cannot receive, because it neither sees him nor knows him; you know him, for he dwells with you, and will be in you. I will not leave you desolate; I will come to you. Yet a little while, and the world will see me no more, but you will see me; because I live, you will live also. In that day you will know that I am in my Father, and you in me, and I in you. He who has my commandments and keeps them, he it is who loves me; and he who loves me will be loved by my Father, and I will love him and manifest myself to him." Judas (not Iscariot) said to him, "Lord, how is it that you will manifest yourself to us, and not to the world?" Jesus answered him, "If a man loves me, he will keep my word, and my Father will love him, and we will come to him and make our home with him. He who does not love me does not keep my words; and the word which you hear is not mine but the Father's who sent me.

John 14.15-24

What does Jesus promise us in this passage?

_____
_____
_____
_____
_____
_____

Jesus then describes how he *must* be crucified in order to bring us into God's presence[a]. What does Jesus say is the ultimate fruit of this suffering in John 15.11, 16.20-22 and 17.13?

_____
_____
_____

We can also see how Jesus death and resurrection elevates his disciples from being "friends" (John 15.15) to members of his "family" (John 20.17), a level of breathtaking intimacy[b]. The next couple of chapters consider *why* and *how* Jesus' crucifixion brings us into God's presence.

---

[a] In these passages Jesus refers to his impending crucifixion and resurrection as his "glorification" and "coming to the Father". Jesus states the central themes of his teaching in John 13-17: love one another as Jesus loves us; have faith in Jesus as the Son of God; his atoning death provide access to God's presence; and that we are powerless to do good apart from him.
[b] See CCC 1997 and 2014.

Joy Beyond All Understanding

By his death and Resurrection, Jesus Christ has "opened" heaven to us. The life of the blessed consists in the full and perfect possession of the fruits of the redemption accomplished by Christ. He makes partners in his heavenly glorification those who have believed in him and remained faithful to his will. Heaven is the blessed community of all who are perfectly incorporated into Christ.

This mystery of blessed communion with God and all who are in Christ is beyond all understanding and description. Scripture speaks of it in images: life, light, peace, wedding feast, wine of the kingdom, the Father's house, the heavenly Jerusalem, paradise: "no eye has seen, nor ear heard, nor the heart of man conceived, what God has prepared for those who love him."

Because of his transcendence, God cannot be seen as he is, unless he himself opens up his mystery to man's immediate contemplation and gives him the capacity for it. The Church calls this contemplation of God in his heavenly glory "the beatific vision":

How great will your glory and happiness be, to be allowed to see God, to be honored with sharing the joy of salvation and eternal light with Christ your Lord and God, . . . to delight in the joy of immortality in the Kingdom of heaven with the righteous and God's friends.

CCC 1026-8

WHAT'S YOUR EXPERIENCE?

1. Do you think you can find joy being in God's presence? Why (or why not)?

_____

_____

_____

_____

_____

2. What might be an obstacle to deeply experiencing God's presence? Why? Think of an example from your own life.

_____

_____

_____

_____

_____

3. How would you characterize your joy of being with God in prayer? Check one of the following phrases or list one of your own:

o "Who me, pray?"

o "Beats washing the dishes"

o "Somewhere between a cheeseburger and a steak"

o "Wow! Nothing I'd rather do"

o _____

4. Describe in your own words God's "ultimate goal" for you:

_____

_____

_____

_____

Whatever our experience of being in God's presence, Jesus promises us access to God, a place of "indescribable and glorious joy", in the words of St. Peter, his leading disciple (I Peter 1.8). We will consider both why there is so much joy in God's presence and how to experience it more in Chapter 4, "Beholding God's Face". Let's first take a look at how Jesus brings us into God's presence in the next few chapters.

You Must Be Joking

But are you convinced such joy even exists? I mean, what could really be better than _____? Aren't I just talking about a self-induced emotional state? The only definitive answer comes from spending time with God yourself in prayer and at Mass.

14

2 - Gaining Access to His Presence

Massacre of the Saints, Rubens

WHAT WENT WRONG?

From our consideration of the "tabernacle parade" and the psalms above, there is little doubt that David and his court found great joy in God's presence. In fact, the psalms describing this joy contain some of the most poetic and beautiful words ever penned. However, this joy soon dissipated as David's heir, Solomon, fell into certain sins including idolatry. The kingdom of Israel itself split and disintegrated as Solomon's sons were caught up in their own destructive patterns of sin. What

> ### Embarrassed going to a Nudist Beach?
>
> Seriously, most of us don't have perfect bodies! Despite even a good diet and exercise, aging inevitably drains our bodies of whatever youthful luster they once had. As aging corrupts our physical bodies, so sin corrupts our souls, making us ashamed before the all-seeing God. Despite their perfect bodies, Adam and Eve grew ashamed of their "nakedness". Read Genesis 3 to see why they are ashamed of their nakedness.

went wrong?

Israel's difficulties are common to us all. So easily we choose a lesser good over the best, such as working late to the neglect of our spouse or putting our kid on a travel team at the cost of family dinners. Sometimes we even do evil despite wishing to do good, like abusing a substance we know will harm us[a]! This tendency common to all humanity can be called our *fallen nature*. Indeed, evil is evil precisely because it destroys. Insulting both hurts the person insulted but also "hardens" the person doing the insulting, making them mean-spirited. After any sin we somehow know deep inside that we have displeased God[b] – at least before we learn to suppress such pings of conscience. Having displeased him, we fear entering his presence until matters are set straight[c].

But our difficulty admitting sins and seeking forgiveness is perhaps the theme of human history – beginning with Adam foisting blame onto Eve, and Eve shifting it to the Serpent. So often we content ourselves with the pursuit of the many good things of creation – which happen to be rather abundant these days – and, like ancient Israel, soon forget about God. In the process our zeal for merely good things tends to get us into more and more trouble.

> ### Sorry is Not Enough
>
> Gene Hackman plays Royal, a long-derelict father of three, in the post-modern, tragic-comedy, the *Royal Tannenbaums*. The movie blames Royal for the neurosis of one son, the suicidal tendencies of the second, and the desperate alienation of his adopted daughter. Subservient to fortune and womanizing, bankruptcy compels the now sixty-something Royal to fake a terminal illness in the hopes of re-ingratiating himself with his family and thwarting a suitor for his estranged wife. Before his family uncovers the charade, Royal's new-found appreciation of them turns his desire for reconciliation earnest, leading him to seek out his daughter:
>
> Royal - Your brother's all torn up inside (who just attempted suicide in despair of her love)
> Daughter - I really don't care to discuss it with you
> Royal - Can't somebody be a shit all their life and then try to repair the damage? I think people want to *hear* that
> Daughter - Do they? You probably don't even know my middle name
>
> Of course, Royal neither recalls that she's named after his mother nor realizes his responsibility for his kids' pathetic wretchedness and Royal's daughter won't let him simply paper over his long absent love. Despite its dry wit and whimsical story line, the story ends realistically with Royal's former wife marrying her new suitor and the reconciliation with his kids merely hinting at what might have been.

Eventually we realize that nothing earthly satisfies our deep hunger for the joy that comes only from God's love and presence[d]. Or we come to deny *the possibility* of such joy and grow cynical. Or, more commonly today, we accept society's fairy tale ending to our lives in which everyone who *tries to be nice* (regardless of their success) is automatically transported into some vague place of bliss known as Heaven. Belief in a "Free Pass to Heaven" conveniently liberates us to

---

[a] See also Romans 7.17-20.
[b] In fact, God reveals some of his fearful holiness, beginning with Moses, in part to help us not to sin! See Exodus 20.18-21.
[c] We have lost that "holiness without which no one will see God", Hebrews 12.14. Cf. CCC 29.
[d] CCC 30.

pursue lesser joys with abandon as long as we *try to be nice* about it. If we should hurt someone along the way, we just *have to be sorry.*

Unfortunately, none of these alternatives has a happy ending, unless you ultimately patch things up with God – for the only true joy comes from being with God and his people (more on this in the next chapter).

Sin Destroys Us and Our Ability to be with God

I think most of us have little idea how terrible sin is until it's too late. We all have seen how divorce ravages a couple and their children, perhaps firsthand. We are all experienced in giving and receiving spite. Many have known the worship of fame and fortune, power and pleasure.

We may fail to realize immediately how a particular sin destroys ourselves or those around us. In fact, just like in Eden, Satan goes all out to attract us to forbidden but deadly  fruit – more accurately, *forbidden* because it's *deadly* fruit[a]. Sometimes, only much later do we learn the harm of a sin.

Sin destroys. God takes such destruction personally since he made us - not for destroying ourselves and others - but to live with Him. Just as God rejoices in being with us, choosing self-destruction displeases Him. Sin disfigures our magnificent beauty and nobility; after all, God made us in his image and likeness[b]! How does the craftsman feel when a hammer mars or shatters his masterwork? Since sin destroys his work, we must ask God's forgiveness!

---

[a] See Genesis 3 and CCC 1708.
[b] Particularly in our freedom, appreciation of goodness, truth & beauty, and our ability for friendship and love. See CCC 1701.

God hates sin precisely because it destroys his own handiwork and ruins *our ability* to enjoy being with him, perhaps even *the awareness* that our greatest joy is found only in him[c]. Sin inevitably, disfigures our personalities, making us more and more selfish and, in a word, *intolerable* to be around! Sin turns our capacity for love and friendship into one for hate and jealousy. We all have been around bitter people. In fact, how easily we can come under the power of sin, be it vanity, pride, anger, bitterness, an addiction, etc.[d]. A paradise of hardened sinners is no paradise at all! The wretchedness of sin renders us unfit for God's presence. Since only God can restore the damage done by sin we must ask for his help! God both must forgive our sins *and* help us to change.

We can't begin to understand the problem of sin until we appreciate how intensely God loves *us* and wants *us* to be with him. He knows and values every hair on *our* head[e]. God desires only what is good for *us*; everything he commands is for *our* good. *We* were made for the greatest of purposes – an eternity of joy with the most kind, enchanting, beautiful, funny, loving, generous, and creative beings – God himself and his family. Indeed, we grieve God by choosing a path of self-destruction that renders us incapable of – and even averse to – a relationship with him and his people.

> ### *See for Yourself*
>
> Take a look at parables of a lost coin, a lost sheep, and a derelict son in Luke 15. What rejoices Heaven?
>
> _____
>
> _____
>
> _____
>
> What angers God? Consider a coach's disappointment over his Super Bowl MVP throwing away his career in a fit of rage. Or how a budding opera diva succumbing to a drug addiction would anger her mentor. But all of us are endowed with greater riches than mere athletic or musical talent: God designed us to live with him, a gift which sin destroys! How would you feel about your son or daughter throwing their lives away?
>
> _____
>
> _____
>
> _____

NICE IS NOT ENOUGH – THE CALL TO PERFECTION

Yeah, but wait a minute, you might say. Isn't the main thing in Jesus' teaching simply *trying to be nice*? Let's take a look. The Sermon on the Mount (Matthew 5-7) summarizes Jesus' moral teaching. What does Jesus say in 5.17-20 about the 613 commands of the Jewish law?

_____

_____

---

[c] See Romans 1.18-21 as to how sin clouds our mind from even seeing the truth about God; cf. CCC 29.
[d] See Romans 6-7 on the power of sin to enslave us.
[e] See Romans 5.8-9, Luke 12.7

18

In Matthew 5.21-48 how does Jesus radicalize "being nice" regarding . . .

v. 21-22: *Anger*

_____

_____

_____

v. 27-30: *Lust*

_____

_____

_____

v. 38-47: *Loving Your Enemy*

A bit of Bluster?
Is Jesus just exaggerating a bit to make his points? Read how Jesus concludes the Sermon on the Mount in Matthew 7.13-14 to see how adhering to his teaching is a matter of eternal consequence.

_____

_____

_____

What's the punch line of this rather "challenging" teaching in Matthew 5.48?

_____

_____

_____

As you can see, Jesus expects much more than simply *being nice* - his expectations truly boggle the mind. God's ambition for us reaches beyond just repairing sin's damage to making us perfect like himself. Indeed, God's own level of holiness and love is our mark. We saw in the last chapter how God desires for us to dwell intimately with him, even as sons and daughters. As members of his family, he expects us to resemble, well, members of his family – that is, to be like the *father of the family*. God calls us to be holy as he is holy![a]. Being with wonderful people – starting with God himself – is what makes heaven so wonderful!

BECOMING HOLY LIKE GOD REQUIRES GOD'S HELP

Sadly, a funny thing happens if Jesus only forgives my sins: I keep on sinning! And even if God repairs the damage of our sins, we still fall well-short of perfection. The sane human response to

---

[a] I Peter 1.15-16 echoes God's earlier commands in Leviticus 11.44-45 and 19.1.

Jesus' call to perfection is:

I Just Can't Do It!

Jesus' radical teaching, in fact, makes us call out for help, driving us to himself – for only He can make us holy and loving creatures. So we cry:

God Help Me!

Fortunately, God gladly gives us the grace to change through the action of the Holy Spirit in our lives. We will consider this transforming power of God in Part II, Chapter 4.

WHAT'S YOUR EXPERIENCE?

1. Describe some destruction from sin you've recently experienced or witnessed (get out the newspaper if you happen to be perfect or live among perfect people).

_____

_____

_____

2. Rather than violating some arbitrary rule, sin harms ourselves and others. Such harm results from violating any of God's laws which can be found in Scripture and the *Catechism*. In your own words, why is God offended by the harm sin does to ourselves and others?

_____

_____

_____

3. In what areas do you struggle most to be good or loving?

_____

_____

_____

THEOLOGICAL SUPPLEMENT:
WHY DID JESUS HAVE TO SUFFER ON THE CROSS?

Perhaps it is easy to see that we *need* God's forgiveness, as discussed above, because sin damages ourselves and others – who happen to be God's creatures, his property, if you will. In particular, sin ultimately destroys our ability to have a good relationship with God and others – which is the source of our greatest joy.

Understanding *how* God forgives us may be more challenging because it involves understanding his justice, which is far more perfect and complete than human justice. It starts with the fact that sin objectively harms ourselves and others - which damage must be compensated. We all have a certain ingrained sense of justice or fairness. If I steal your car, I can hardly expect a friendly greeting next time we meet. Rather, I have to return your car and probably make further amends before I venture anywhere near you, let alone hope to resume our friendship! In many instances, however, we are jaded to the damage of a particular sin, such as cheating on our taxes or viewing pornography, and we fail to see any need for compensation or retribution. But God is all-seeing and perfectly just, necessitating objective compensation for every sin, which is precisely what Jesus provides for us on the Cross[b].

God's justice, mostly beyond human reckoning, requires payment or "atonement" for sin. Fully understanding the intensity of God's love for us, his hatred of sin, and the requirements of *divine justice* may be possible only when we are with Him in heaven. What we know now is that God hates how sin destroys us and our ability to be with Him. And that God effects the forgiveness of sin by paying back "all the cars we have ever stolen" with something infinitely more valuable than all the "stolen cars" put together – the *life* of his own Son, sacrificed on the Cross.

Another perspective on how Jesus pays for our sins is that in Baptism, we are literally "joined" to the person of Jesus (hence the reality of Christians as making up the "body of Christ"). The

---

Jesus, the BEST of Friends

Jesus is better than your average friend! What kind of love does Jesus shows his friends in John 15.13 ?

_____

_____

Jesus *fulfills his disciple's joy* by going to the Father – *by way of the cross* (John *17.13*), indeed, the very next day. His love for them and us required such a death.

---

[b] See Romans 3.23-26, Hebrews 10.11-22 & 12.14, CCC 599-623, and "For Further Study" .

penalty for sin is eventually dying and being excluded from God's presence[a]. Since Jesus, God's only begotten Son, never sinned, Jesus immediately resumes fellowship with the Father upon rising from the dead. In a sense, Jesus does offer us a Free Pass to Heaven: by putting our faith in Jesus, Baptism – our explicit statement of faith[b] – joins us both to Jesus' death and resurrected life with God:

For if we have been united with him in a death like his, we shall certainly be united with him in a resurrection like his. We know that our old self was crucified with him so that the sinful body might be destroyed, and we might no longer be enslaved to sin. For he who has died is freed from sin. But if we have died with Christ, we believe that we shall also live with him. (Romans 6:5-8)

---

[a] Romans 5.12 and I Corinthians 15.56.
[b] Our parents speak on behalf of baptized infants, who later "affirm" their faith in Christ during Confirmation. See CCC 628 & 1214 (Baptism) and CCC 1289, 1298 (confirmation).
[f] See also Romans 3.23-25 and the CCC references in the For Futher Study section.

3 - Choosing Joy: Accepting the Father's Mercy

For God so loved the world that he gave his only Son, that whoever believes in him should not perish but have eternal life. For God sent the Son into the world, not to condemn the world, but that the world might be saved through him

John 3:16-17

Jesus coming down from the Cross, Van Dyck

JESUS IS THE ONLY ANSWER TO THE PROBLEM OF SIN

Jesus died on the cross to pay for our sins and to re-establish our relationship with God. Was there any other way for God to grant access to the place of eternal joy for which he made us? In a word, no. Even if we fail to appreciate the true wretchedness of sin's destruction and how much our sins offend Him who made us God tells us that sin is *the problem* that prevents us from entering into the joy he intends for us.

There's a bit of history of God attempting all kinds of things with ancient Israel to address the sin problem. God had already sent a lot of great moral teachers. He had already given a Law that spells out holiness. He had already erected a system of sacrifice that, among other things, required sacrificing one's choicest property to signify even a minor sin's destructive force. He had raised up a great and holy king. He had built an elaborate temple whose architecture and ritual symbolized his holiness. Ultimately, all of these efforts end in failure to solve the problem of sin, although they certainly teach any observer that sin is a barrier to being with a holy God.

A more radical solution is required – the sending of a perfect teacher of incarnate, absolute holiness. An awesomely holy king of kings. Even more so, the sending of a

> "I am the way, and the truth, and the life; no one comes to the Father, but by me."
>
> John 14.6

perfect priest offering the ultimate sacrifice that is more precious than any possession – the life of God himself. In Jesus, we learn of the true holiness God requires and through his forgiving sacrifice[f] our sins are wiped away and we become fit to receive God's own Holy Spirit. It is all so terribly and wonderfully true. God sent his own son to die for us because *there was no other way* – and because *he so deeply loves us* and *desires us to be with him and his people*. We affirm this truth at each Sunday Liturgy where together we proclaim the Nicene Creed[a]:

> *For us men and for our salvation . . . for our sake*, he was crucified under Pontius Pilate; he suffered, died, and was buried. On the third day he rose again . . .

Read Luke 18.9-14. What is the one thing we have to do for God to extend his mercy to us?

_____

_____

_____

Actually, we all do this every Sunday at beginning of each Mass[c] and again later when we proclaim our belief in Jesus saving power to forgive our sins in the Gloria:

> Lord Jesus Christ, only Son of the Father, Lord God, Lamb of God, *you take away the sin of the world: have mercy on us*; you are seated at the right hand of the Father: receive our prayer.

---

[a] These truths are also expressed in all the Eucharistic Prayers of the Mass. In fact, the Mass taps into the grace released on the Cross – see CCC 1382.

[c] In the Penitential Rite and the *Kyrie*, respectively, where we first confess our sinfulness and then, as a group, ask for God to have mercy. Finally, before receiving communion we ask for God's mercy in the Agnus Dei (Lamb of God).

GOD REALLY LOVES US, BUT THE CHOICE IS OURS

Behold, I stand at the door and knock; if any one hears my voice and opens the door, I will come in to him and eat with him, and he with me.

Revelation 3:20

Do you want to be with God? God calls to us, but the choice is ours. God pursues us, woos us, and does everything he can to draw us to himself. Jesus wept over Jerusalem, knowing how few in that day would respond to his invitation[a].

How great is heaven's joy when we accept his invitation? Jesus says that it is like the joy of a father regaining a son who was headed towards a tragic end. Sometimes we just need to experience the misery of life to grow receptive to God's offer. Read Luke 15.11-32 about the Prodigal Son. What makes the younger son decide to return to his father's house?

_____

_____

_____

_____

_____

The Prodigal Son, Rembrandt

The younger son knew something of his father's tremendous love for him that gave him hope to return despite the deep injury his departure must have inflicted upon his father. What would have become of the younger son had he never turned back?

_____

_____

_____

Does the father's response surprise you? What does it tell us about God's love?

_____

_____

_____

---

[a] Luke 19.41.
[c] John 8.1-11.

Turning to God with our Whole Lives

> The kingdom of heaven is like treasure hidden in a field, which a man found and covered up; then in his joy he goes and sells all that he has and buys that field.
>
> Matthew 13:44

The key phrase here is "in his joy". The man recognizes a stunning bargain. He *gladly* sells everything to possess a priceless treasure. God offers us the ultimate source of joy: life with him and his people. On one hand, life with God is free for the asking. On the other hand, we have to want it more than everything else in the world!

Part of the "everything" we possess actually blocks us from God, namely, sin. Jesus forgives a woman about to be stoned to death for adultery, but tells her to sin no more[c]. Jesus calls us to repent, or turn away from, sin[a] precisely because of how sin destroys and prevents our access to God, as discussed in Chapter 2 and to accept Jesus' offer of salvation and eternal life with God. St. Peter takes up these themes in the finest first sermon in the history of preaching shortly after Jesus rose from the dead, provoking the crowd to ask how they should respond, to which Peter answers:

> Repent, and be baptized every one of you in the name of Jesus Christ so that your sins may be forgiven; and you will receive the gift of the Holy Spirit.
>
> Acts 2.38

A full 3,000 people took the plunge of Baptism that day, signifying their repentance and acceptance of God's offer of forgiveness and eternal life! To baptize means "to immerse in water", a water through which the Holy Spirit cleanses away our sins[b] and literally incorporates us into the body of Christ, so much so, in fact, that St. Paul almost always refers to his fellow believers as those who are "*in* Christ".

What else does "sell everything" mean? Well, if you sell your house, empty your savings and retirement accounts, sell off your furniture, computer, and your other belongings, you've emptied your life of everything. Then you trade the resulting pile of money for a relationship with God. It's sort of like emptying out a glass of dirty water in order to fill it up with champagne.

Jesus does not intend for most of us to literally "sell everything", however, but uses this figure of speech to describe how life with God requires us at the cost of our independence and autonomy to embrace completely his plan for our lives and to live by his power. As you can see, Jesus calls us to turn our whole life over to him throughout the gospels:

---

[a] Jesus makes turning away from sin, i.e., "repentance", the central theme at the outset of his ministry (Matthew 4.17, Mark 1.14-15,38), at its conclusion (together with forgiveness, Luke 24.46-7), and emphatically throughout. For the latter, see Jesus' message of "repent or perish" in Luke 13.1-5, his warning to unrepentant cities in Mathew 11.20-24 to the current generation in comparison to Nineveh in Matthew 12.38-42.

[b] CCC 1238. See the excellent more general discussion of Baptism in CCC 1213-84.

Giving Our Life to Jesus

Ask for Help & Forgiveness
- Ask, seek, knock (Mt 7.7-11)
- Ask for mercy, like the tax collector (Lk 18.9-13)
- Seek Jesus like the paralytic lowered through roof (Mk 2.1-11)
- Ask for Jesus' help like the repentant thief (Lk 24.40-43)

Repent and Believe
- Repent from sin (Mt 4.17, Mk 1.14-15, Lk 13.1-5)
- Believe in Jesus and obey his teachings (Jn 12.46-48)
- Believe the gospel and be baptized (Jn 3.1-8)

Make Jesus Lord of Our Life
- Sell everything to buy hidden treasure (Mt 13.44)
- Sell everything to buy pearl of great price (Mt 13.45)
- Give up one's life (Mt 10.39, 16.25-26)
- Renounce everything (Lk 14.33, cf. Mt. 19.16-22)
- Choose God or money (Mt 6.19-21, 24)
- Love Jesus more than family (Mt 10.35-37)
- Take up one's cross (Mt 10.38, 16.24)

Obey Jesus' Commands, Become like Jesus, Love Others, Share Jesus
- Keep Jesus' commands (Jn 14.15)
- Follow Jesus' teaching in Sermon on Mount (Mt 7.21-27)
- Be perfect as your heavenly Father is perfect (Mt 5.48)
- Love one another as Jesus loves us (Jn 13.34)
- Feed the hungry, cloth the naked, visit the imprisoned, etc. (Mt 25.31ff)
- Proclaim the gospel of repentance and faith in Jesus (Mk 16.15-16)

It's a little scary, isn't it? In order to save our life, we must lose it. Jesus promises us that the life we gain will be infinitely better than the one we lose, one ultimately characterized by indescribable joy. He promises to make us perfect but only if we follow him completely and draw upon God's power, the Holy Spirit.

---

d The door to Heaven will eventually "shut", Luke 13.22-29; cf. Matthew 7.13-14.

We each have only a limited time to make our choice. Failure to embrace life with God leaves us locked out forever from his presence[d] – left prey to the other angels and men who have opted out. The cruel history of humanity and perhaps our own lives – to speak nothing of the Bible - warns us against the absolute misery of those who opt out. For in God is the fountain of life, in his life, we see light (Psalm 36.9), the very source of goodness, truth, beauty, love, joy and peace.

Read the Parable of the Rich Man and Lazarus in Luke 16.19-31. In what ways does God, while respecting our free will, try to bring us home to an eternal life of joy with him?

_____

_____

_____

_____

Why Reject the Father's Love?

"God is the infinitely good and merciful Father. But man, called to respond to him freely, can unfortunately choose to reject his love and forgiveness once and for all, thus separating himself for ever from joyful communion with him. . . [Hell] is the state of those who definitively reject the Father's mercy . . . the state of those who freely and definitively separate themselves from God, the source of all life and joy."

John Paul II (*L'Osservatore Romano*, 4 Aug 99; cf. CCC 1033)

WHAT'S YOUR EXPERIENCE?

1. Do you know how much God wants you to be with him and how happy that will make him? Do you ever feel like the Prodigal son? How do you feel about the welcome home in store for us, if we choose to come home?

_____

_____

_____

_____

2. Perhaps you have "been away" from the Father's house or have neglected to follow God's commandments and direction for your life. If this is the case, repent and ask God's forgiveness

right now. Go to confession before the week is out. Right now, or before you go to bed tonight, fall on your knees before God and renew your Baptismal promises by responding "I Do" to the following questions[b]:

- Do you reject sin, so as to live in the freedom of God's children?
- Do you reject the glamour of evil, and refuse to be mastered by sin?
- Do you reject Satan, father of sin and prince of darkness?
- Do you believe in God, the Father almighty, creator of heaven and earth?
- Do you believe in Jesus Christ, his only Son, *our Lord*, Who was born of the Virgin Mary, was crucified, died, and was buried, rose from the dead, and is now seated at the right hand of the Father?
- Do you believe in the Holy Spirit, the holy Catholic Church, the communion of saints, the forgiveness of sins, the resurrection of the body, and life everlasting?

3. In what ways does Jesus' all-encompassing call to discipleship and holiness challenge you? (See page 25)

_____

_____

_____

_____

As Jesus' disciples, we come to our Master daily in prayer– even throughout the day – simply to enjoy his presence but also to draw on his power to be like him. We will look more closely at daily personal prayer and worship in the next several chapters. In participating in the Mass, we also worship God together as a people and directly participate in the forgiveness of Jesus' sacrifice and power to live as holy and loving people. Worship in the Mass will be taken up in a separate study, *Made for Worship*.

The Church's Prayer of Absolution

God, the Father of mercies, through the death and resurrection of his Son
has reconciled the world to himself
and sent the Holy Spirit among us for the forgiveness of sins;
through the ministry of the Church may God give you pardon and peace,
and I absolve you from your sins
in the name of the Father, and of the Son, and of the Holy Spirit.

---

[b] Catholics do this each year at the Easter Vigil Mass. Actually, something along these lines is a very good thing to do every day by deliberately saying the Lord's Prayer with Jesus' Lordship particularly in mind – "your will be done" or reciting the Apostles or Nicene Creed with its acclamation of Jesus as the "One Lord". Meditating on the scripture passages such as those on page 25 is also very helpful.

30

4 – Prayer: Beholding God's Face

Landauer Altar, Albrecht Dürer

How lovely is your dwelling place, O LORD of hosts!
My soul longs, indeed it faints for the courts of the LORD;
my heart and my flesh sing for joy to the living God

Psalm 84:1-2

TYPES OF PRAYER

Need or anxiety drives many of us to pray. "Oh God – Help!". Asking for help is a fine thing – God loves to help us. But how about when we don't particularly need something? As my Aunt Pat says, just like with any other relationship, if you want a relationship with God you have to spend time with him.

In fact, having a relationship with God is the whole point of Christianity! Yes, of course, God transforms us, empowers us with his Spirit, and pours his love into our hearts so that we love those around us. And even when we aren't particularly enthused, we still strive to love those around us and resist temptations, e.g., do the laundry, be nice to the grumpy neighbor, look away from the soft-porn commercials, etc. Even so, at the end of the day, our primary goal is simply to be with God and his people.

The three components of prayer all directly relate to being in God's presence[a]. **Contemplation** involves basking in the warmth of God's love as well as gazing upon his beauty and glory and, in beholding his face, seeing the personification of love, mercy, justice, goodness and God's other attributes. **Thanksgiving** is the natural response to beholding God's goodness to us. **Intercession** is also our natural response to perceiving God's will, which can be best understood by spending time with God in prayer and reading Scripture. Of course, you don't have to be in God's presence to thank him or intercede – but it helps! This chapter considers contemplation, while Chapter 5 examines thanksgiving and intercessory prayer. Chapter 6 looks at some general helps and models for prayer.

The ultimate contemplative prayer is what happens when we stand before God in heaven. Church tradition refers to this as the beatific vision:

> This mystery of blessed communion with God and all who are in Christ is beyond all understanding and description. Scripture speaks of it in images: life, light, peace, wedding feast, wine of the kingdom, the Father's house, the heavenly Jerusalem, paradise: "no eye has seen, nor ear heard, nor the heart of man conceived, what God has prepared for those who love him."   CCC 1027-9

---

[a] Above all, prayer involves "a vital and personal relationship with the living and true God" (CCC 2558); and "the life of prayer is the habit of being in the presence of the thrice-holy God and in communion with him" (CCC 2565). Of course, the Mass is the pre-eminent prayer of the Church. These chapters, however, are primarily concerned with personal prayer rather than corporate worship. The excellent discussion of prayer in the *Catechism of the Catholic Church* identifies several categories of prayer that I have implicitly grouped under Contemplation: Blessing and Adoration and Praise. Transformational prayer, as discussed above, as well as seeking God's particular guidance for our life can both be considered aspects of intercessory prayer. Again, this whole chapter is worthy of a more extended practical treatment which is planned as another title in this series. Of course, much more can be said about Scripture reading, study and memorization. See www.GodsPlanForYourLife.org for a resource listing and links.

It's easy to think that contemplative prayer outside of heaven is limited to monks and nuns who devote their entire lives to prayer, locked away in monasteries. And yet the Church teaches that all Catholics should taste at least some of the sweetness of God's love and beauty (Ps. 27.4; 34.8), despite the rough and tumble of studying, raising children, being married, working, and generally living in a busy world filled with many pressing demands and absorbing distractions. Indeed, John Paul II requires that parishes become schools of prayer, where "the meeting with Christ is expressed not just in imploring help but also in thanksgiving, praise, adoration, contemplation, listening and ardent devotion, until the heart truly 'falls in love'"[a].

If contemplative prayer is a foretaste of being with God in heaven, then it is a foretaste both of experiencing his love, tenderness and committed-ness to us as beloved sons and daughters of the Father, brothers and sisters of the Son and spouses of the Holy Spirit. Prayer can equally be a foretaste of the wonders and incredible joy of beholding God's splendor. Fully entrusting ourselves to God and placing our lives in his hand opens up our hearts to the warmth of his love. As our emotional temperaments vary one to another our affective experience of God's love varies. For one it may be the feeling of absolute serenity, for another the sweetness of being forgiven. For some, a certain unfathomable inward joy, for others a quiet serenity or confidence. Some will experience the "jubilation" of King David dancing before God, other the quiet glow of adoration. One person's experience of God's love may vary from day to day and from season to season. Some may be so damaged by personal sin that it takes many years to learn to trust God and begin experiencing the richness of his love.

Success in developing and experiencing some level of contemplative prayer depends on the following factors (among others):

1 – having a vision and an understanding of contemplative prayer
2 – developing a hunger for being with God
3 – adopting and maintaining a habit of daily prayer
4 – maintaining a minimal level of sanctity by repenting of any and all sin on a daily basis and accessing redemptive and regenerative grace through attending Mass and Confession.

The purpose of this chapter is to help develop a rudimentary or very basic level of contemplative prayer, particularly as it relates to beholding God's splendor. I believe that most people should find with some regularity a sweetness and delight in God's presence by praying contemplatively on a daily basis, even if such prayer is as brief as fifteen minutes and involves only the simple steps discussed in this and the following chapters[b]. Of course, there is much, much more that God has for some of us in this life and all of us in heaven. It is worth noting that sustaining a

---

[a] *Novo Millenio Ineunte* 33. Contemplation is used a bit more broadly in this chapter and includes aspects of praise and adoration.

[b] One might say that this chapter is about "basic contemplation" and speaks especially of aids to contemplation. It is important to remember that true contemplation is a gift from God. However, there are many thing we can do to prepare ourselves to receive this gift.

lifetime habit of even fifteen or twenty minutes of daily prayer depends upon putting God first in our life and giving him free reign to make us holy and loving like himself, in very practical and tangible ways, some of which are discussed in Part II of this book on ongoing conversion (or discipleship).

Embracing even a simple prayer life supported by a lifetime of discipleship yields joy in prayer and a slow but steady transformation into the very likeness of God. As C.S. Lewis notes, God is making us beings of dazzling brilliance, filled with a holiness and love resembling his own. Indeed, we are becoming "partakers of the divine nature" (II Peter 1.4). To be sure, for most of us this transformation will take a lifetime and our "unutterable and indescribable joy" will be complete only in heaven. And yet here and now God lavishes on us foretastes of heaven and our access to him and his transforming power is limited only by our desire.

---

[i] See II Corinthians 4.6 *inter alia*. Due to its limited scope this study primarily considers God's beauty; in a sense, to the extent God's other attributes are attractive we consider them beautiful. Glory, *kabod* in Hebrew and *doxa* in Greek, has a parallel though somewhat different connotation than beauty and also captures some of the overall character of God. Philosophically, the word sublime is often used to mean something akin to spiritual beauty. See pages 15-28 of David Hart's *The Beauty of the Infinite* (Grand Rapids/Cambridge: Eerdmans, 2003) for a rigorous discussion of how to define beauty. You may also consult pages 34-45 (and beyond) of von Balthasar's magisterial *The Glory of the Lord: A Theological Aesthetic, Vol. I, Seeing the Form* tr. by Leiva-Merikakis, Fessio and Riches (San Francisco: Ignatius, 1982).

CONTEMPLATING GOD: BEAUTIFUL BEYOND DESCRIPTION

Rejoice always, pray constantly, give thanks in all circumstances; for this is the will of God in Christ Jesus for you.   I Thessalonians 5.16-18

God is said to be beautiful and glorious beyond description: out of Zion the perfection of beauty, God shines forth (Ps 50.2). In addition to experiencing God's love, contemplation involves gazing upon God's beauty and glory[i]. Contemplating in the sense of recognizing and enjoying God's beauty and glory may involve as little as five or ten minutes of prayer or "gazing". Of course, contemplation can also verge on the mystical, where one becomes completely absorbed in beholding God, even for long stretches of time. This chapter is concerned with everyday, shorter and less intense moments of enjoying God which are available to all Catholics during their times of personal prayer and in sacramental worship.

Let's begin by trying to get to the bottom of our own experiences of beauty, which may help us to contemplate God's beauty. So take some time to consider what you find beautiful – at least five minutes in some quiet place, close your eyes and think about beauty, about persons, things, and experiences or whatever you associate with beauty. Jot down what comes to mind in a free-flowing manner. Use the writing space in the back of this booklet. Only after finishing that exercise turn back to this page to complete the questions and reflections below.

Describe your greatest encounters of beauty over the last several months[a]

---

[a] This question may be a bit of a stumper for many since we are often too caught up in our everyday lives to notice beauty – just put down anything that comes to mind and revisit this question after reading through the rest of the chapter.

1. _____
   _____
   _____

2. _____
   _____

3. _____
   _____

Beauty has a certain element of mystery to it – why are mountains beautiful?   Describe why chocolate tastes good and I'll tell you why something's beautiful!   Beauty is just beautiful, like chocolate is simply delicious. So, what is God's beauty like?

Suppose your greatest encounter with beauty is a sunset over the ocean. Way better than a mud puddle, right? Well, that sunset is like a mud puddle compared to God's beauty! Or to compare the beauty of a cooing baby with gazing on the Father is like comparing a candle to the sun.

The same type of analogy holds for God's other attributes, such as his love, goodness, mercy, power, knowledge, creativity, and justice. Can everyday experiences tell us something about God's characteristics? Consider a mom rescuing her baby from a burning house as a very pale comparison to God's love for us and parents denying themselves luxuries and even necessities in order to save for their kid's college tuition as one for goodness. Magnifying such love a gazillion times gives us some idea of God's love for us and to what extremes he will go for our sake.   Consider some everyday experiences that, by comparison, can help us understand some of God's attributes:

- ➤ Loving   __*changing my baby's diapers*_____
- ➤ Kind   _____
- ➤ Good   _____
- ➤ Merciful   _____
- ➤ Powerful   _____
- ➤ Knowing   _____
- ➤ Creative   _____
- ➤ Just   _____
- ➤ Awesome   _____
- ➤ Glorious   _____
- ➤ Funny   _____
- ➤ Humble   _____
- ➤ Holy[a]   _____

Well, God is the ultimate version, quite literally the personification, of each of these adjectives, all at once! We are all attracted to kind faces, just people, awesome sights. In heaven we will see kindness, justice, and awe itself, literally emanating from the face of God, together with all his other attributes.

A good way to contemplate God is by considering his goodness, love, humility, etc. and then praising these divine attributes over and over again. I often begin worshiping God by simply saying over and over again, "God you are so _____", filling in the blank with one of God's attributes. I repeat the phrase slowly and meditatively (silently or out loud, whatever is more comfortable). Sometimes I imagine the saints and angels of God surrounding his throne together chanting the same phrase in worship, thousands upon thousands.

As you grow in your life of prayer and ask God for more and more of his Holy Spirit, and he will reveal to you more and more of his beauty and glory.

---

[a] Holiness simply describes God as being utterly different or apart. One synonym is being "godlike" or "godly". In a certain way, the perfection of all of God's other attributes make up his holiness.

IMAGINE BEING IN HEAVEN

To take a different perspective, picture being in heaven with God for a few minutes. After all, if prayer is being with God, in heaven is where we see him face to face. So thinking about heaven can help our prayer life on earth. How do you imagine heaven?

Two Angels, Raphael

1. _____

2. _____

3. _____

Perhaps the most vivid account of eternal life with God in the Scriptures is found in Revelation 4.1-11. What's going on in heaven, according to this passage?

_____

_____

_____

_____

_____

What the saints and doctors of the church tell us is that, at least to a limited degree, God wants us to enjoy the same sweetness of gazing on his holiness and grandeur, the radiant beauty of all his attributes, that we see the saints and angels enjoying in heaven here in Revelation. I can't tell you mechanically how God brings us this wonder and sweetness. What I do know is that when we prayerfully think about God's goodness and beauty, somehow the Holy Spirit makes us see and even experience it! This is true whether we are praying privately in the morning, entering into worship at Mass, meditating upon the rich mercy of Christ in reciting the Rosary, singing worship songs,

---

Worship in Spirit?

Jesus said to her, "Woman, believe me, the hour is coming when neither on this mountain nor in Jerusalem will you worship the Father. You worship what you do not know; we worship what we know, for salvation is from the Jews. But the hour is coming, and now is, when the true worshipers will worship the Father in spirit and truth, for such the Father seeks to worship him. God is spirit, and those who worship him must worship in spirit and truth." John 4.21-24

---

reading about God's holiness in Scripture or looking at icons.

The last several chapters of Revelation further describe what the heaven will be like. List five important things about heaven described in Revelation 19.1-9, 21.1-7 and in 21.22-22.5:

1. _____

_____

2. _____

_____

3. _____

_____

4. _____

_____

_____

5. _____

_____

In addition to basking in God's love, heaven will dazzle and mesmerize us with his glory and beauty – of which we shall never tire or have enough. In fact, the Lord wants us to experience this joy, *to some degree*, right now, in both our personal prayer life and our life of corporate worship centered on the Mass.

Can our contemplation of God *really* be like gazing on Him in heaven? Yes and no. No, probably not on any kind of regular basis; even St. Paul only sporadically experienced being "caught up into heaven" in his prayer. After all, the Lord gives us each responsibilities and entrusts us with his mission while we live on earth (as we shall further investigate in the chapters ahead). Yet we can experience *imperfectly* at least some of the joy of being with God in heaven.

HUNGRY? At the end of the day, how richly and deeply we contemplate God is proportional to how badly we wish to be with Him. The more deeply we wish to see God, the more God reveals himself. We have to translate our desires into the practical steps outlined in the next section. God is there for the asking but, again, we do have to ask.

> ### Worship at a Rock Concert?
>
> As a sixteen year old I idolized the musician Eric Clapton – together with tens of millions of adoring fans around the world. Together with 40,000 fans, I chanted his name - Clapton, Clapton, Clapton – longing, hungering for an encore. After soaking up this adulation many long minutes backstage, Clapton finally sprang through the haze of smoke and dazzling lights onto stage. The chanting erupted into shrieks and frenzied clapping until well into the encore song.
>
> Compare adulation of rock stars with Revelation 4.

As we spend more and more time with him, God transforms us into his own likeness, that of Jesus. Ultimately, he so changes us that an irrepressible love for others and hunger to draw them to God supplements, and even replaces, loving others out of obligation. An overwhelming desire to be with God replaces praying out of a sense of duty. Just as Jesus loves spending time with the Father, so will we.

HELPS IN CONTEMPLATIVE PRAYER

The practical exercises above considering God's beauty and other attributes and what heaven will be like are primers for contemplation; hopefully they help cultivate our sense of what is beautiful (and glorious). Let me summarize a few more practical pointers:

1. Take the time to seek God: **ask God to bring you closer and to help you simply to be with him, to experience his love, and behold his beauty and glory; ask God to pour out his Holy Spirit** – his very presence - on you. You can do this right now; you may also find some help from your parish's prayer group.
2. Meditate and **consider how much God loves us**. Consider how he draws us to himself as discussed in the first three chapters of this book. Read through the gospels and seek out books on God's love at your local Catholic bookstore.
3. We need to **let God change us** – it may take a while before we are pining and longing for God's presence all the time. Practice makes perfect. Consistency is important. Keep on praying and seeking God on a daily basis, even when we don't see direct fruit. Developing a solid prayer life takes time!
4. **Sing worshipful songs**. A fine singing voice isn't necessary to worship God in song. Find a few songs that you particularly like, get the music, and begin a personal prayer time by singing. Sing softly if you are embarrassed or to avoid distracting others. St. Augustine famously teaches: he who sings prays twice.
5. **Set aside some time for silence**, to simply be with God and listen to him. You may wish to find a beautiful spot or a quiet place.
6. **Pray through God's attributes**, as discussed above, taking just one or two at a time, considering the ways in which God so fully exemplifies the attribute, all the while praising God over and over again, slowly: "God, you are holy"; or "God your power is without measure"; etc.
7. Using an approach similar to praising God's attributes, **pray through the titles of God** as found in Scripture. Consult your local Catholic bookstore for one of the many books on this topic as well as on God's attributes[a].
8. **Pray through the Psalms**. Read through them and note ones that you particularly like. The Liturgy of the Hours, based on the Psalms, is also a brilliant method.

My own experience of contemplative prayer has been fed by two primary sources: reading and meditating on Scripture and receiving the outpouring of the Holy Spirit through the Charismatic Renewal. I usually sing worshipful songs to begin a time of contemplation. Though everyone may not feel drawn to charismatic prayer, the Holy Spirit is given to all of us in baptism and

------

[a] A simple listing of God's titles may be found online at : http://www.jesuswalk.com/ebooks/pu_names-god_list.htm.

confirmation (e.g., John 1.32-33, Acts 1.4-5, 2.1-4, 10.43-48). The Holy Spirit dwells in us (e.g., John 14.17, Romans 8.1-17, and I Corinthians 6.19) and is our access to God's presence in prayer (e.g., John 4.23-24, II Corinthians 3.16-18). In other words, the Holy Spirit is the basis for contemplative prayer[a] and we should continually seek to be filled more and more regardless of our interest (or lack thereof) in charismatic gifts. Let's make our own John Paul II's daily prayer: Come Holy Spirit.

I believe that asking for and receiving a greater outpouring of God's Spirit provides us something of an initial shortcut to the deeper experience of God in prayer that is described as contemplation. Yet, even if God plunks you down in the middle of the heavenly feast, how easily does everyday life and our own sinfulness interrupt such delight. The foundational work described by the great mystics such as John of the Cross and Teresa of Avila has to be done some how or other, sooner or later, in order to establish a robust contemplative life. See the For Further Study section.

Part II, Chapters 3-8 summarizes God's foundational work of transforming our lives to become like Christ's, which, in turn, deepens and perfects our appetite and ability to contemplate (and be with) God.

WHAT'S YOUR EXPERIENCE?

1. Pick one of your encounters with beauty you listed earlier in this chapter. Describe what you found beautiful. What particularly appealed to you?

_____

_____

_____

_____

_____

2. Which of God's attributes most attracts you? Why?

_____

_____

_____

_____

_____

_____

---

[a] Cf. *Novo Millennio Ineunte* 32-33, which describes our conversation with Christ as being "wrought by the Holy Spirit" and eventually renders us persons "vibrating at the Spirit's touch".

3.   What do you most look forward to about Heaven?

_____

_____

_____

_____

_____

5 - Prayer: Thanksgiving and Intercessory

Vatican Altar Piece, Raphael

THANKSGIVING PRAYER

*Rejoice always, pray constantly, **give thanks in all circumstances**; for this is the will of God in Christ Jesus for you.*   I Thessalonians 5.16-18

Thanksgiving prayer, like contemplative prayer, most naturally flows from being in the presence of God. Rather than appreciating his beauty and glory, thanksgiving is the response of acknowledging God's goodness. The basic human reflex of thanksgiving is what happens if a truck stops at your house and somebody unloads twenty bags of gold at your door: who do I thank? As we stand in God's presence, we recognize his many fabulous gifts to us and – at least on a good day[a] – overflow with thanksgiving.

What to give thanks for? The answer to this question is in many ways the key to life. If we don't have a foundational awe and appreciation of God's creation – beginning actually with ourselves,

---

[a] . . . and on a bad day? Give thanks anyways! The reality of prayer is that we will always be fighting distractions of many types. Press on despite your headaches. Over time, our battle with distractions diminishes.

whatever our circumstances or limitations – we're probably not going to get very far in our relationship with God. God made us conscious – aware of our self and, more importantly, of God. He made us capable of appreciating goodness, truth and beauty. Finally, as discussed in Chapter 3, he invites us into an eternity of joy with him – for which he personally pays the price and into which he personally guides us. Oh, and did I mention giving us the Holy Spirit?

We may enjoy rather pleasant earthly circumstances or be a quadriplegic (or caring for one). We may have appeared on the Oprah Winfrey show as the Victim of the Year. Doesn't matter in the eternal scheme of things. God invites us to an eternity of joy. The transitory and perhaps quite difficult nature of our circumstances only further highlight God's incredible offer to us. Looking to eternal life with God isn't a cop-out or crutch for those facing great challenges – it's the answer to why we all experience suffering sooner or later: adversity focuses us on the eternal joy of life with God. Adversity also strengthens our faith and stimulates growth toward moral perfection (James 1.2-4).

So whatever our circumstances God both invites us to an eternity of joy with him and has destroyed the only thing blocking us, sin. That alone should fuel an eternity of rejoicing and thanksgiving. Especially if we live in the West where our lives are probably packed at least with *good things* if not *good relationships*. We realize how many blessings we have once we stop feeling like we

> **Dad's Death**
>
> As I complete the writing of this book, I grieve the loss of my father who died just ten days ago. My relationship with dad went from pretty good to nearly ideal during the sixteen months he battled cancer. There's no room for anger at the premature loss of my father - only gratitude to God over the incredible gift he was to us.

"deserve" a bigger house, a better job, a car that doesn't break down, kids that don't cry, etc. The key to gratitude is treating every good thing or relationship as a gift (again, start your list with the items discussed in the above paragraphs). Don't dwell on gifts that haven't been given or are provided only temporarily.

HELPS IN THANKSGIVING

I will give thanks to the Lord with my whole heart . . . I will be glad and exult in you.

Psalm 9.1

Especially if you haven't done much by way of thanksgiving prayer, I suggest simply listing out the many ways God blesses you. The following is a guide for preparing such a thanksgiving list:

1. Start with being made in His image and likeness. Nay, start with existing at all (and continuing to exist at this moment)! Being made like him has most to do with the capacities for self awareness, for recognizing goodness, truth and beauty (and their opposites), for the

deep joy related to truth, goodness and beauty and much less to do with our physical and intellectual abilities (or lack thereof).
2.   Having a personal relationship with God.
3.   God's work in establishing that relationship through the death of Jesus and giving us the Holy Spirit.
4.   Our families.
5.   Our relationships, particularly fellow believers.
6.   Our material provisions and physical and mental gifts.
7.   Blessings particular to our life.

Now take some time to create your own list:

❖   _____

❖   _____

❖   _____

❖   _____

❖   _____

❖   _____

❖   _____

❖   _____

❖   _____

INTERCEDING – FOR THE KINGDOM OF GOD

*Rejoice always, **pray constantly**, give thanks in all circumstances; for this is the will of God in Christ Jesus for you*   I Thessalonians 5.16-18

"Prayer" generally refers to communicating with God but is also used more narrowly to mean petitioning or interceding. Intercession, like contemplation and thanksgiving, involves accessing God's presence both to be heard but also to learn what God wants to happen. In fact, we should intercede only for what we think or know God wishes or wills[a]. We don't just intercede as "free lancers" or "independent contractors", but as priests of the most high God – not in the *persona Christi* (the person of Christ) as an ordained priest does while celebrating the sacraments – but by virtue of being a member of God's people, which as a group is a royal priesthood and a holy nation[b]. The power of our intercessory prayer comes directly from being part of the body of Christ – the ultimate high priest. As we saw earlier, God weeps and rejoices over whether or not people choose to embrace the fullness of his life and plan for them. As intercessors, we stand with God and pray for God's will for various situations and people. As we behold God's face we also most clearly see his will. While contemplation is our response to God's beauty and glory and thanksgiving to his goodness to us, intercession is our response to his love for others.

Our heavenly father loves us and wants to give us good things!!!! Ask him for your needs and for good things.[c] Above all, pray for God's will to be done, which in the long run is always for the best.

Seeking God's will and simply listening for his voice is an important area of prayer in its own right. Ask God questions! Oh Lord, what job do you wish me to have? What do you wish to teach me in this difficult situation? . . . And don't just ask, but also listen.

> ## Lord, Teach us to Pray . . .
>
> *Our Father, who art in heaven,*
>
> 1 *Hallowed by thy name*
> 2 *Thy kingdom come*
> 3 *Thy will be done, on earth as it is in heaven*
>
> 4 *Give us this day our daily bread*
> 5 *And forgive us our trespasses as we*
>   *forgive those who trespass against us*
> 6 *Lead us not into temptation*
> 7 *But deliver us from evil*

Sometimes God will want us to use our own judgment to figure things out, other times he may himself speak to us quite clearly. When I was considering what to do after graduating from college, I had several options that made sense in human terms but I felt a strong conviction that God wanted me to live in a particular city, which ruled out all options but one!

---

[a] Romans 8.26-27; Matthew 6.10; CCC 2610-11.
[b] I Peter 2.5, CCC 1546-7. Cf. CCC 901-3.
[c] Matthew 6.25-33; 7.7-11.

Another major area of intercession is actually asking God to make us like himself. This may be called *transformational prayer*, the substance of which will be considered in Part II of this book, "Ongoing Conversion".

I know this all sounds a bit grandiose and ethereal. In practice, however, prayer is rather earthy until we gain heaven. Our lives are fraught with distractions and disorders, hardships and interruptions. Yet, despite all the difficulties of making prayer happen on a daily basis, we can possess no greater joy than simply being with God. Being with God is what we are made for. When we are with God, we do things like contemplate his beauty and glory, rejoice and give thanks over his many blessings to us, and participate in his active love for others. Thank God - otherwise, prayer wouldn't be worth all the bother.

Intercession in Amsterdam

That morning, I happened to be scanning for new radio stations when I came across a talk show promotion of a "Big Sex" sweepstakes for a five day all-expense paid trip to the red-light district of Amsterdam. This shocking promo was still ringing in my ears when Steve – an old friend and business associate - looked at me confidentially and said, "I've got to tell you what happened *to me* in Amsterdam". We had been talking about Christianity, which Steve stopped practicing in childhood, and I dreaded some unseemly revelation.

With nothing to read one night while there on business boredom led Steve to play a "fan and stop" game. Finding a Bible tucked away in a desk, Steve fanned its pages and plopped his finger down in the middle of the page he opened to – right on his own name!

The one in a million odds got his attention. The shock lasted for days and Steve eventually told a work associate. Steve's even greater shock was learning this man had been praying daily for God to reveal himself to Steve!

PRAY FOR PEOPLE

Concerning intercession, the first step is seeking God for his will and purposes regarding our needs, people we care for, and other matters related to the material and spiritual condition of those around us. Even without any advanced discernment, we can be pretty sure that God wants everyone to come into the joy of a relationship with himself and other people and to satisfy all of their material needs. In fact, examine Luke 11.5-13. What does the Lord expect his disciples to pray for?

_____

_____

_____

_____

HELPS IN INTERCESSION

Beyond a few generalities, there are no ready-made checklists for intercession. Primarily think about and list what is best for yourself and other people *from God's perspective*. I suggest keeping a notebook or prayer journal for this purpose (or pda or word file). For starters prepare a list in the following space:

Person   Petition

❖ _____   _____

❖ _____   _____

❖ _____   _____

❖ _____   _____

❖ _____   _____

❖ _____   _____

❖ _____   _____

As you pray through this list, ask God to reveal his will more fully even as you ask Him to act for the benefit of the persons on the list.

A simple formula for intercessory prayer? Open (or close) your time of intercession with the Our Father. Then pray through your list. Set aside several times a week to go through the whole list. You will be surprised at how quickly your list grows into a page or two. You will also be surprised at how God answers your prayers. Close with a Hail Mary.

> *Hail Mary, full of grace.*
> *the Lord is with thee and blessed is the fruit of thy womb, Jesus.*
>
> *Holy Mary, Mother of God,*
> *pray for us sinners, now and at the hour of our death.*

Many people who pray the rosary use it as a way of interceding. In particular, state your intentions in a prayer before you begin the rosary, for example, "Oh Heavenly King, I ask for such and such . . . Mary, I ask you to intercede to the Father for these matters". Then be mindful of particular intentions while you recite the meditative prayers of the rosary. Remember, you are not piling up prayers[a] or just performing some duty in praying the rosary, but entering into a rhythm of meditative and intercessory prayer[b].

---

[a] Matthew 6.7.
[b] CCC 2673-79; 2708.

LIVING THE LIFE OF PRAYER

1. What are your reasons for making time for daily prayer and Scripture reading?

   _____

   _____

   _____

   _____

   _____

2. What would you have to change in your schedule to pray or read Scripture for 15-30 minutes per day (or to make it to daily Mass)?

   _____

   _____

   _____

   _____

   _____

3. Find a couple or small group of people with whom to intercede. Have each person pray an intention out loud, e.g., "Lord, we pray that Jane and Paul's marriage would be restored". Then allow a full minute or two for the other people to repeat the prayer in their own words, either silently or out loud.

   _____

   _____

   _____

   _____

   _____

6 - Prayer: Let's Get Practical

Mary, Albrecht Dürer

But when you pray, go into your room and shut the door and pray to your Father who is in secret;
and your Father who sees in secret will reward you.
And in praying do not heap up empty phrases as the Gentiles do;
for they think that they will be heard for their many words.

Matthew 6.6-7

So what are the practical steps involved in experiencing God more deeply in prayer? This section will describe some of the biggies: maintaining holiness; making time for prayer; and finding prayer styles or methods that work for you. In addition, there are useful "helps" in terms of how to go about intercession, thanksgiving and contemplative prayer and a "recipe" for getting started.

HOLINESS

There are some important preliminaries. Namely, you have to wear the right clothes (so to speak). You have to be clothed in the holiness of God, to have the smelly repugnance of our sinfulness washed away[a]. The price of such a cleaning? Just ask for forgiveness – but you have to ask. The way to keep clean? Ask for help – in fact, become a habitual asker for help. Seek God's grace through the sacraments and by asking him to give more of the Holy Spirit. This incessant posture of pleading for God's help is the sense of the "pray constantly" in the I Thessalonians 5.16 passage.

Sinning and failing to ask God's forgiveness blocks and undermines our personal prayer. That's one of the reasons why spiritual writers through the ages recommend a daily examination of conscience, i.e., scrutinizing yourself for ways in which you may have offended God or others or failed to love and serve others.

> ### Worship with Reverence and Awe
>
> [18] For you have not come to what may be touched, a blazing fire, and darkness, and gloom, and a tempest, [19] and the sound of a trumpet, and a voice whose words made the hearers entreat that no further messages be spoken to them. [20] For they could not endure the order that was given, "If even a beast touches the mountain, it shall be stoned." [21] Indeed, so terrifying was the sight that Moses said, "I tremble with fear,"
>
> [22] But you have come to Mount Zion and to the city of the living God, the heavenly Jerusalem, and to innumerable angels in festal gathering, [23] and to the assembly of the first-born who are enrolled in heaven, and to a judge who is God of all, and to the spirits of just men made perfect, [24] and to Jesus, the mediator of a new covenant, and to the sprinkled blood that speaks more graciously than the blood of Abel.
>
> [28] . . . Let us offer to God acceptable worship, with reverence and awe; [29] for our God is a consuming fire.
>
> Hebrews *12*

---

[a] CCC 2813.

TOO BUSY TO PRAY?

Want to die . . . spiritually and eternally? Read John 4.10-15 and John 7.37-39. What do you think Jesus means by living water? How does this apply *to you*?

_____

_____

_____

_____

Why does Jesus compare prayer to going to the well in a desert society without plumbing?

_____

_____

_____

_____

DOING IT

What's the basis for a good prayer life? In a word, doing it! Not talking about it, not reading about it, not thinking about it, but doing it – and doing it regularly. If you want a good prayer life – don't just go on a retreat or read a book – start praying on a daily basis for fifteen minutes. Realistically, you may need to start with five or ten minutes per day. Start with a minimum that you can manage every day.

Did I already mention the need to actually pray? To pray daily? *My advice is to give up on personal prayer unless it becomes your #1 daily priority.* Otherwise, the press of daily life will quickly dissolve our prayer life into a good intention soon forgotten! The reality is that spending time with the Lord every day is our greatest gift and privilege, not just our Lord's command. Did I already mention that being with Him

> ### Mary's Choice
>
> See Luke 10.38-42 for the story of Mary & Martha. What does Mary choose for?
>
> _____
>
> Why does Jesus praise this choice?
>
> _____
>
> _____
>
> _____

is the ultimate source of joy and happiness? The Lord guarantees that everything will work out fine – actually, as well as it can – if we spend time daily with him. It doesn't matter how pressed we are by the demands of our life (although maybe some of our priorities need to be adjusted). Of course, we must be responsible to our family, job or studies, health, etc. I promise you that

God ultimately works everything out way better than we can begin to imagine if we make prayer our top daily priority.

SET SOME GOALS

How much time to pray? Your goal will vary according to your particular situation. Most people might eventually build up to ½ hour per day of prayer or more, perhaps starting out with only five or ten minutes. John Paul II spent one hour in personal prayer in addition to praying a set of psalms and related prayers (the Liturgy of the Hours) and celebrating Mass every day. Many people find that first thing in the morning is the best time for prayer.

Once you're tucked in?

A good friend of mine shared that his best time for daily prayer "is when I get really comfortable, right before bed. In fact, I get in bed and shut my eyes. Its automatic. I can't imagine not praying at that time". Just as I was mentally rescheduling my daily prayer to so desirable a time slot, my friend added, "the only problem is, I only pray for two minutes before falling asleep".

Making room for prayer may require listing and analyzing your priorities. If prayer is your number one priority, which lesser priorities must yield time to daily prayer? Where is the best place in your daily and weekly schedule to fit in prayer? Have you ever laid out for yourself a daily schedule? Like with most things, go ahead and explicitly ask God for help. Ask God to free up the time for prayer and simply to get you started.

So, what's it going to be for you? Take five minutes right now to consider a daily prayer time. How much does God want you to pray? What parts of the day work best for prayer? What is a sustainable prayer time on a daily basis – five minutes? Fifteen minutes? One-half hour? Where is the best place for prayer? Your bedroom? Your office/study cubicle? Taking a walk? A chapel? Ask God to give you wisdom and direction in setting the following goals:

Time for daily prayer: _____ (minimum)

to _____ (target)

Location: _____ (preferred spot)

_____ (backup spot)

When: _____ (preferred time)

_____ (backup time)

ACCOUNTABILITY

New Years resolutions are quickly forgotten. An excellent way to boost our success in reaching our prayer goals is to make ourselves accountable. In high school football, by joining the team you make yourself accountable to the coach to make the practices and to work hard. The coach challenges and pushes you to be successful, offering praise and encouragement. You are ashamed to run wind sprints at a trot.

Make yourself accountable to your spouse, a friend, or a small group to make your prayer goals. Encourage each other. Challenge each other. Of course, making ourselves accountable to each other is simply harnessing a natural force. We don't like to fail. Having to admit failure to others can be a powerful incentive to hit our goals. While accountability may help you to get in the habit of praying, never lose sight of the real reason for prayer: simply being with God.

METHODS OF PERSONAL PRAYER

Just as we have different personalities, we also have different spiritual temperaments[a]. Some of us will do well by singing and speaking to God out loud. Others will find silent prayer best. Some find the Liturgy of the Hours a very fruitful form of prayer. Others write out their prayers in prayer journals. Most find at least some regular reading and meditation on God's Word in one form or another indispensable. Some memorize Scriptures, others find Eucharistic Adoration very powerful, and some combine both! All the varieties of personal prayer are not easily listed.

Most people with a regular personal prayer life rely on several different forms or methods of personal prayer. The trick is finding out which work best for you, and, then, of course, actually using them on a daily basis! Whatever methods and patterns you choose, our daily and weekly rhythm should include large portions of thanksgiving, intercession and contemplation. You should also be mindful in exploring prayer styles that "there is no other way of Christian prayer than Christ . . . our prayer has access to the Father only if we pray 'in the name' of Jesus"[c].

Whatever your prayer method, I can't emphasize enough asking God to reveal himself and develop our relationship with him. Ask God to pour out his Holy Spirit upon you. In imitation of many holy people I have known and because of its success, daily I pray for more of the Holy Spirit:

> Come Holy Spirit,
> Fill the Hearts of the faithful.
> Enkindle in us the fire of your love.
> Be with me all day! Help me to be holy and loving.

---

[a] See the section on Personality and Piety, pages 45-73, in *Invitation to a Journey* by M. Robert Mulholland, Jr. (Intervarsity: Downers Grove, 1993).
[c] CCC 8664.

THE WORD OF GOD IN PRAYER

Let the Word of Christ dwell in you richly   Colossians 3.16

Scripture has a special role in almost all forms of prayer. God speaks to us through the Bible. The Bible's caretaker, the Church, urges it upon us forcefully![a]. Justly famous is the saying of St. Jerome, a father of the Early Church:

Ignorance of Scripture is Ignorance of Christ.

The Bible is *designed* for use in all aspects of our prayer life. The Psalms, in particular, are the preeminent Christian prayer book[b]. Use the Psalms for thanksgiving, intercession and contemplation. Worship God by praying passages such as the Song of Moses (Exodus 15) and the Canticles of Mary & Zechariah (Luke 1). Meditating on Scripture allows the word of God to work in us (I Thess 2.13), to make its home in us (I John 2.14) and to help purify our hearts (Hebrews 4.12). God speaks to us and feeds us through Scripture reading[c].

I recall shortly after my faith awakening as a freshman in college opening my bible after a late evening of study and finding the words of Scripture coming alive to me. It was Jesus speaking *to me* in the parables. The powerful unfolding and richness of the life of the early church recounted in the Acts of the Apostles was the most riveting of dramas. I even found the story of creation compelling! Sure, I had read these passages before but without the eyes of enlivened faith.

THE BEGINNER'S BOAT

You are in one of two boats. Some of you are in the beginners' boat where the primary prayers in the past have been the SOS variety – hollering for help when you are about to drown (which may be one of the reasons why God permits adversity in the first place!). I suggest that beginners spend a lot of their initial prayer times simply asking God to reveal himself more and more to

---

[a] CCC 2653.
[b] cf. CCC 1174-78; 2585-89.
[c] Cf. CCC 2705-8.

you. Meditate on the truths covered in Chapters 1-3. Look up some of the *Catechism* and Scripture references in the body of this book and in the "For Further Study" section. Make Jesus more completely lord of your life. These chapters contain ample material for developing thanksgiving prayers; they also will get you started on contemplative prayer.

If you are in the beginners' boat, start with the following recipe, then experiment and vary it over time as you find ways of praying that best suit you.

1. Daily Prayer
   a. Begin by reciting a favorite psalm or passage from the bible (perhaps one from this study).
   b. Spend 5-10 minutes in **Thanksgiving** to God for his goodness to you, praying through your thanksgiving list developed in Chapter 5.
   c. Spend 5-10 minutes of considering God's beauty and glory (**Contemplation**).
      i. Think comparatively about some of the things you described as beautiful above. As an example, "God, you are more beautiful than a sunset on the ocean" or "Your love is far richer than that of my own parents". You could also recite favorite psalms.
      ii. Another strategy is to praise the different attributes of God: "Oh God, you are full of mercy"; "Oh God, you are so loving".
      iii. Whatever you verbalize should be done very slowly . . . let the words hang in the air.
      iv. It often helps to imagine heaven or simply what Jesus is like. We don't "imagine" our relationship with God; rather, we put ourselves in a frame of mind to meet God. You will continue praying because God indeed will fill you himself, with a joy that is indescribable and makes you *know* the completeness and reality of simply being with God.
   d. Spend 5-10 minutes **Interceding**.
      i. As you start out, a large proportion of your prayer time will be devoted to asking God to change your life and fill you more and more with his Holy Spirit - starting with establishing a personal prayer time! Praying for God's power to be at work in us must become a basic habit of life, ideally prayed nearly as often as we breath, permeating our days rather than merely beginning our designated "prayer time". The fruit of this prayer, coupled with surrendering our will to God, is the transformation in Christ described in Part II of this book as well as power to love others as God loves us.
      ii. Pray through your intercession list developed in Chapter 5.

2. Scripture Reading/Study Every Third Day (or so)
   a. Begin with 5 minutes of prayer (following b-c above, or simply praying)
   b. Spend 10-25 minutes reading, studying & meditating on Scripture.
      i. Begin with the Gospel of Luke and continue with the Acts of the Apostles.

ii. Continue with following the readings that are used for Sunday Masses (and daily, if time permits) (see "for further study" for a few websites and references).

3. In addition to Sunday Mass, attend daily Mass once during the week instead of taking a personal prayer time[a].

THE SEASONED SAILOR'S BOAT

If you have the good fortune of praying regularly, you might evaluate your prayer time along the following lines:

1. Questions of Consistency
   a. Are you praying at least 15 minutes per day? Pray about whether God wants you to expand that time to 30 minutes or more.
   b. Are you asking God for the Holy Spirit to come down on you daily?

2. Questions of Focus
   a. Is your main, overarching objective in prayer simply to be with God? (think about it, there are many other worthwhile, but lesser, objectives for prayer)
   b. Whatever your particular habits or forms of prayer, over the course of the week are you spending substantial time giving thanks, interceding, and contemplating? What about "transformative prayer"? (see intercessory prayer above)
   c. How much Scripture are you reading each week? Do you have a general study and reading plan?

YOUR PRAYER TIME

Indicate below the pattern of prayer you are shooting for by filling in the blanks.

Sample

	MON	TUES	WED	THURS	FRI	SAT	SUN
TYPE	Prayer	Prayer	Mass	Prayer	Scripture	Prayer	Mass
PLACE	Den	Den	St. Paul	Den	Den	Starbucks	St. Rita
TIME	7 am	7 am	Noon	7 am	7 am	8 am	11 am
DURATION	:15	:15	:40	:15	:20	:30	1:15
BACKUP TIME	10 pm	10 pm	10 pm	10 pm	?	?	n/a

---

[a] And every day, if possible. Both going to daily Mass and taking a prayer or Scripture time (like the Holy Father) may be the ideal, but we live in the real world of time constraints, schedules and logistics. Of course, you have to decide the best mix for yourself. On the one hand, the Church emphasizes the importance of personal prayer and Scripture reading by devoting one of the four sections of its *Catechism* to prayer. On the other hand, the Church holds up the Eucharist as the source and summit of your faith.

Yours

	MON	TUES	WED	THURS	FRI	SAT	SUN
TYPE							
PLACE							
TIME							
DURATION							
BACKUP TIME							

Keep in mind that your schedule will change from time to time and you will need to adjust the above plan. You may wish cut this out and paste it on your mirror or some other place; or keep it in your wallet as a reminder. You can download blank forms from www.GodsPlanForYourLife.org or simply write out your own.

WHAT'S YOUR EXPERIENCE?

1. What kinds of prayer are you most comfortable with? What types of prayer would like to explore?

   _____

   _____

   _____

   _____

2. What are your greatest obstacles to daily prayer? How can you overcome these?

   _____

   _____

   _____

   _____

Your Guarantee

Our daily prayer time is essentially the birthright of every Christian: God gives us this time with himself regardless of how demanding and busy are our lives. Sort a like a "free pass" for daily prayer – God guarantees that we will never get "penalized" for praying fifteen minutes a day!

Embracing God's Plan for Our Life

PART II: ONGOING CONVERSION

"COME, FOLLOW ME"
—— BEING A DISCIPLE ——

1 - Discipleship is Following God's Plan for Our Life

*4**He chose us** in him before the foundation of the world to be holy and blameless before him in love. 5**He destined us** for adoption as his children through Jesus Christ, according to the good pleasure of his will, . . . 10**as a plan for the fullness of time**, to unite all things in him, things in heaven and things on earth.*

Ephesians 1

Jesus invited the first disciples to "come, follow me". The notion of discipleship implies a change as we abandon our own plans – probably deeply influenced by society - and follow Jesus' plan. Jesus forms our life anew – not just "spiritually" but also in a very concrete and practical manner. Disciples of the Lord Jesus should, and will, look different than people formed in a worldly way. This chapter introduces the three main components of God's plan for us: conversion; transformation and mission. The beginning of this book considered conversion while the end of this chapter reflects further upon conversion from the perspective of the U.S. Bishops' pastoral

writing. The next chapter takes up the key impediments to following Jesus: the world, the flesh and the devil. Chapter 3 and 4 consider the twin engines of discipleship: God's grace and our effort. The rest of the book then examines the specifics of God's plan for making us like Jesus and loving others as God does.

> ### The Meaning of Life
>
> Jesus lays out the meaning of life (and his death) in chapters 15-17 of John's Gospel. Read John 15.11 and 16.20-24. Describe in your own words what the basis for this joy might be.
>
> _____
> _____
> _____

THE WORLD'S PLANS

American culture brims with plans for every facet of our life starting with when, if and how you are made. Public schools educate and instill "values"; the media and video games decimate your attention span. Take Big Gulps then let Atkins shed your fat. Soft porn TV shows; hard porn only clicks away. If it *feels good*, do it! Big toys for big boys. Consume your way to happiness then let a lawyer shred your credit card debt. Give your all to get ahead but no hard feelings if you get canned. *You're entitled to a good life!*

Kids activities first, second and third, even as your marriage falls apart. Just find what you are really good at, and do it. Smarts, hard work and good looks. Stay connected. Multi-task. Quality time with the family *over a TV dinner*. Work hard, play hard. Just do it: you are *what you do*. The main thing is that you try to be nice and that you feel good about yourself – it's all in your head. You just need some anger management. Therapy and pills. It's OK, as long as you aren't hurting anybody. *Don't Worry, Be Happy.*

> ### Rich Man, Poor Man
>
> I was dazzled by the possibilities opening up to me. I could be fabulously rich – I knew it. I had just finished the novel *Rich Man, Poor Man* by Irwin Shaw when I was in about ninth grade. Somehow I took away from the book that I could accomplish anything I set my heart to, a notion my parents also emphasized. What was I going to be when I grew up? *Successful.* Success became the overriding objective in my life.

Indeed, our culture and society has suggestions and plans for who we are, what will make us happy, our purpose in life, how to relate to other people, what to value, how to shape the basic patterns of our day, and how to make major life choices. Catholics are hardly immune to cultural suggestions on what to do and who to be.

How many guys plan their weekends around watching football games or other sporting activities? How many begin Saturday morning with a time of prayer, bible study, or Mass, even at the expense of watching only part of the football game or playing nine holes instead of eighteen? A comparable set of questions apply to ladies. Unless we deliberately chose how to approach our leisure time, work, marriage, child rearing, etc., we have probably adopted the world's approach by default.

Consider some of the plans or ideas that American culture has for us. List several worldly approaches for the following areas:

Pleasures
> _____
> _____

Being Successful
> _____
> _____

The Perfect Spouse
> _____
> _____

Personal Appearance
> _____
> _____

Getting Ahead	> _____
	> _____
The Perfect Child	> _____
	> _____
Free Time or Leisure	> _____
	> _____

More on the "world" in the next chapter. Suffice it to note here that much that the world offers is illusory and fails to provide deep, long-lasting joy.

GOD'S PLAN FOR OUR LIFE

All things were created through him and for him.

Colossians 1.16

God made you with very specific ends in mind. And he made us in such a way that when we pursue these objectives, we find great joy. Seeking deep happiness or joy is something like a "homing" instinct that pushes and guides us towards God. Following God's plan for our life yields the truest and deepest joy, which plan has three major elements: being with him and his people, becoming like him, and loving who he loves.

Although God tailors his plan to exactly who we are, these basic goals are the same for every human being. First, he made us in order to have a relationship with us. Go no further – this is the purpose of our life. This is why God made us free. This is why he made us the greatest kind of creature; God made us just like himself, in his image. God may have a *gerbil* for a pet but he wants *us* as a member of his family. So being with God also puts us in a brotherly and sisterly relationship with all his other sons and daughters.

He made us like himself so that he could have the best possible kind of persons in his family. Hmmm. Stop to think about it and one notices that even on a good day, most of us little resemble God, at least as revealed in the person of Jesus. I'm not sure that I would want to be in a family for all eternity made up of people like myself, at least such as I am today. The second overall goal in God's plan for us, in fact, is to **make us become like Jesus**.

As God helps us become like Jesus, not only do our characters come to resemble Jesus in holiness, attractiveness, kindness, lovingness, lovability, and so on, but what we love and the things for which we work naturally become what God loves and those things for which God works. **Loving whom God loves** is the third goal in his plan for us.

EMBRACING GOD'S PLAN FOR OUR LIFE: *MAKE JESUS LORD*

> *If you confess with your lips that Jesus is Lord and believe in your heart that God raised him from the dead, you will be saved.*   Romans 10.9

Now the six million dollar question: How do we embrace God's plan for our life? The answer has two parts. First, we must surrender our lives to Christ, exchanging our plans for his plans. Secondly, we must learn the specifics of God's plan through prayer, listening to Scripture and drawing on the wisdom of the Church.

Consider life as one of Jesus' first disciples. Entering into a master-disciple relationship, we move with him throughout Galilee and back and forth to Jerusalem. As a member of a group numbering less than twenty or thirty, Jesus gets to know us quite well. Experiencing Jesus' tremendous love and goodness reveals what life with God is like: knowing Jesus is knowing the Father. This is the defining relationship of our life, one that comes before all others. Being so close to Jesus over a three year period forces us to measure our self against Jesus' character and holiness, his warmth and love, and the quality of his friendship towards us. His example of how to be human, what to do and for what to live is irresistible. Jesus' perfection and goodness reveals one's cheapness and poverty of life; one either flees his presence or pleads for his help!

As our master, he challenges, critiques and disciplines us. Jesus means business and requires absolute obedience. While free to sever the master-disciple relationship at any time, we want Jesus' help no matter what the cost. Jesus sees us through to the goal of becoming perfect like our heavenly father, as our master but sympathetic and warm.

Jesus' first disciples meet the radical call to holiness of the Sermon on the Mount only by surrendering themselves completely to his lordship. Our master's absolute commitment to transforming us, however difficult the task, with a gentle firmness is enormously encouraging. Anything less from Jesus and we would give up before we got started. The power radiating from him converts our intentions into concrete changes in our lives. By the end of a few years, we grow very much like Jesus, becoming filled with the Holy Spirit.

Jesus' lordship transforms us into creatures who naturally finds our highest joy in loving him and his people, as he pours God's love into our hearts through the Holy Spirit (Romans 5.5). He transforms us only after gaining our permission. Our permission essentially amounts to following his direction, being with him, and drawing on the power he so graciously and abundantly provides. Want such transformation and joy? Say "yes" to Jesus. Given the persecution of being thrown out of the synagogue or, eventually, being fed to the lions, Jesus' first disciples often paid a steep price. The cost of following Christ today, while not bloody, still involves our whole lives. Take some time to consider the meaning of Jesus' words:

So therefore, whoever of you does not renounce all that he has cannot be my disciple.

Luke 14:33

Application Question #1 - How can you apply Jesus' words to your life? List some specifics.

_____

_____

_____

Have you made Jesus lord of your life? There is no better time than right now. For myself, I find that I need to consciously re-assert Jesus' lordship over my life every day. Pray simply,

Oh God, I give my life fully to you without reservation: I am yours. Be lord of my life
Take me, hold me, do with me as you see fit.
In the name of the Father and of the Son and of the Holy Spirit, Amen.

If Jesus is our Master and Lord, we embrace his plan for our lives – but what does this mean practically? First of all, a life of prayer, as discussed in Part I, chapters 4-6. The rest of this chapter introduces the three general processes through which we embrace God's plan for our lives.

SPECIFICS OF EMBRACING GOD'S PLAN FOR OUR LIFE

The general goals of God's plan for our life are to be with him, to become like him and love whom he loves. How does God use his Holy Spirit, Scripture, the Church, the sacraments, the lives of the saints, our small group and other tools to bring this about? God's work of implementing his plan for our life can be broken down into three processes:

Conversion	God brings us into a relationship with himself and his people when we repent and accept forgiveness
Transformation	God makes us like Jesus, in terms of holiness and being filling us with his empowering Spirit
Embracing Mission	God infuses us with his Power to love others by caring for their needs, evangelizing them to Christ, and by serving within the Church

The rest of this chapter will concisely review the process of conversion covered at the beginning of the book, this time following the description of the U.S. bishops. The next three chapters consider how to overcome roadblocks to God's plan and, beginning in chapter 5, the balance of the books considers transformation and embracing mission.

CONVERSION BRINGS US INTO LIFE WITH GOD AND HIS PEOPLE

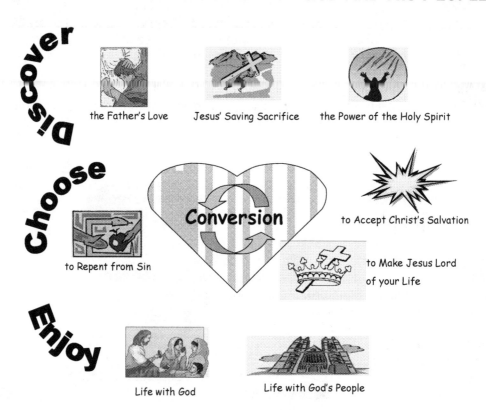

Discover
the Father's Love
Jesus' Saving Sacrifice
the Power of the Holy Spirit

Choose
to Repent from Sin
Conversion
to Accept Christ's Salvation
to Make Jesus Lord of your Life

Enjoy
Life with God
Life with God's People

We have already discussed conversion in Part I, chapters 1-3. By way of review, let's consider how the U.S. Bishop's pastoral letter on adult faith formation describes conversion:

> At the heart of all we are and do as the Church is a revelation of great Good News: God, who is love, has made us to enjoy divine life in abundance, to share in the very life of God, a communion with the Holy Trinity together with all the saints in the new creation of God's reign. Faith, which is a gift from God, is our human response to this divine calling: it is a personal adherence to God and assent to his truth. Through searching and growth, conversion of mind and heart, repentance and reform of life, we are led by God to turn from the blindness of sin and to accept God's saving grace, liberating truth, and sustaining love for our lives and for all of creation.[x]

Give some thought to how you would explain conversion to a non-believer or to a confused and hardly practicing or non-practicing Catholic.

1. Describe the most central truths of the Gospel.

_____

_____

_____

_____

_____

_____

2. What steps are necessary to embrace life with God?

_____

_____

_____

_____

_____

The archetypical conversion story is that of the Apostle Paul. Read Acts 26.9-18. Paraphrase verse 18 in your own words.

_____

_____

_____

_____

_____

Application Question #2 - Few of us have such dramatic conversions. Describe how you experienced conversion – discovering or re-discovering our relationship with Jesus - as an adult. Try to describe your conversion in terms of several steps.

Step #1

_____

_____

_____

Step #2

_____

_____

_____

Step #3

_____

_____

_____

Step #4

_____

_____

_____

2 – What's Stopping Us?

Consider St. Paul's description of life prior to having a relationship with Christ, when we were "spiritually" dead:

> *You he made alive, when you were dead through the trespasses and sins in which you once walked, following the course of this **world**, following the **prince of the power of the air**, the spirit that is now at work in the sons of disobedience. Among these we all once lived in the passions of our **flesh**, following the desires of body and mind, and so we were by nature children of wrath, like the rest of mankind.* Ephesians 2.1-3

Most of the New Testament writers discuss the world, the flesh and the Devil (the "prince of the power of the air") as three forces that undermine our being with God, let alone becoming like Jesus and loving whom he loves. As Christians, we must contend against these forces throughout our life on earth. Let's take a closer look.

THE WORLD

The "world" is used in Scripture in two distinct senses. The first sense is morally neutral and refers to all human beings, as in "For God so loved the world, that he gave his only son" (John 3.16). The second sense in which world is used in Scripture has clearly negative connotations, referring to the society and culture – and especially its embedded values – of all those who have not accepted God's plan for their lives, as in John's admonition to love not the "world" (I John 2.15).

The fact is that almost everyone who hasn't accepted God's plan for their lives has one of their own. While these plans may involve pursuing good things, they often do so in a warped or exaggerated way, one which ultimately distorts us and undermines our happiness. Consider consumerism, i.e., a hyper-emphasis on the acquiring consumer goods. We all know people subtly (or not so subtly) dominated by the desire to have a big house, car, vacations, etc.; a pursuit doomed to failure. Since only God is capable of filling us with the true joy and happiness pursuing anything else dooms us to trying futilely to draw joy out of dry holes or putrid wells. Sex is another example. God imbues sex with a certain often rather wonderful pleasure, but sex fails to quench our appetite. So if you don't know any better (and perhaps even if you do) – a fixation on sex turns your spouse into an object of gratification undermining intimacy and friendship. Or how easily can our quest for sexual gratification lead resort to lying or manipulating another person, whether we are married or single?

> **Love not the World**
>
> Do not love the world or the things in the world. If any one loves the world, love for the Father is not in him.   I John 2:15

Or consider developing a child's potential. While it's wonderful to see your child cultivate their gifts and accomplish much, how easily can such efforts undermine the time you actually spend relating to them and their happiness becomes wed to how much they accomplish? Or take work, or leisure, or one's appearance, or, just about any good thing. Sometimes when people fail to wrench satisfaction out of good things, they try evil ones. The world has all kinds of ideas and plans for making us happy – all of which are doomed to failure.

Application Question #1 - In what specific areas have you most experienced the World's influence?

_____

_____

_____

_____

_____

The World and the Devil: What Catholics Believe

408 The consequences of original sin and of all men's personal sins put the world as a whole in the sinful condition aptly described in St. John's expression, "the sin of the world". This expression can also refer to the negative influence exerted on people by communal situations and social structures that are the fruit of men's sins.
409 This dramatic situation of "the whole world [which] is in the power of the evil one" (1 John 5:19; cf. 1 Peter 5:8) makes man's life a battle:

> The whole of man's history has been the story of dour combat with the powers of evil, stretching, so our
> Lord tells us, from the very dawn of history until the last day. Finding himself in the midst of the battlefield man
> has to struggle to do what is right, and it is at great cost to himself, and aided by God's grace, that he succeeds
> in achieving his own inner integrity. (Vatican II, *Gaudium et Spes*, 37 §2).

2852 "A murderer from the beginning, . . . a liar and the father of lies," Satan is "the deceiver of the whole world."

Catechism of the Catholic Church

THE "FLESH"

To make matters worse, our own sins and those of others affect us even after we repent! Sin deforms and destroys who we are – and we have all sinned. The damage of sin often takes a while for God's grace to restore. Much of the damage is to our power to choose. Since God makes us free, he provides help only as we ask: failing to ask makes it infinitely more difficult to receive his help. Our old habits of choosing poorly (sinning) are often called "the flesh" or "the old man" in Scripture. Impatience

> *True Story*
>
> The glee and joy of kindergartners is infectious. You're part of the game, no questions asked, tumbling from one delight to the next. "But what happens by the time they reach middle school?" wondered the young seminarian helping out as a grade school gym teacher. "The bright faces had mostly grown long for my eighth graders. The world, the flesh and the devil have a way of beating us up and stealing our joy".

sometimes frothing over into temper loss is probably my own biggest ongoing struggle against the flesh. Read Galatians 5.13-26. How does Paul describe the influence of the "flesh" [a]?

_____

_____

_____

_____

If you wish to be with God, you must allow him to transform you by living by his Spirit. Notice how deadly the works of the flesh can be in v. 21?

Application Question #2 - What areas of the flesh do you struggle with most?

_____

_____

_____

_____

THE DEVIL

To make matters even worse, in addition to human beings the "world" includes spiritual powers and angels, who pursue their own plans for being happy. Unfortunately, those who reject God's plan generally fall prey to an age-old happiness substitute: dominating others! Scripture refers to the king of these would-be rulers as Satan. Consider Jesus' experience in Luke 4.1-13.

Over whom does Satan rule? Do you think Satan exerts the same power today?

> ### Spiritual Warfare?
>
> For we are not contending against flesh and blood, but against the principalities, against the powers, against the world rulers of this present darkness, against the spiritual hosts of wickedness in the heavenly places.
>
> Ephesians 6.12

_____

_____

_____

_____

Does Satan give up after Jesus resists his first temptation? What should that teach us?

_____

_____

_____

---

[a] "Flesh" is translated in the Jerusalem Bible as "unspiritual"; see the brilliant analysis of the usage of flesh in the extensive note to Romans 7.5 in the Jerusalem Bible.

In John 13.2 and 14.30, we see that Satan keeps an eye on things and swayed Judas into betraying Jesus into the crucifixion. Check out Gibson's *The Passion of the Christ* for an interpretation of Satan's role in trying to destroy Jesus. Or attend your parish's Holy Thursday and Good Friday liturgies.

Don't believe in evil spirits today? Consider the twenty-plus million who died of genocide in the last century. Look at the work of Al Qaeda. Better still, look at how many little suggestions you experience to be nasty, lust after money, etc. Ever get really scared?

Among the many forces driving our culture, Catholics believe a significant force strives to undermine God's plans for our lives:

> Satan or the devil and the other demons are fallen angels who have freely refused to serve God and his plan. Their choice against God is definitive. They try to associate man in their revolt against God. (CCC 414)

In fact, the Church understands that the last petition of the Our Father is specifically directed against this enemy to God's plans:

> In this petition, evil is not an abstraction, but refers to a person, Satan, the Evil One, the angel who opposes God. The devil (*dia-bolos*) is the one who "throws himself across" God's plan and his work of salvation accomplished in Christ.
> (CCC 2851)

Scripture and Catholic teaching often refers to the influence of Satan and the negative influence of the fruit of men's sin in culture and society as the influence of the *World*. You cannot just say "the Devil made me do it" – the point rather is that a Catholic disciple of Christ must carefully examine whether his life corresponds more to God's plan or to his own plan or the world's.

OUR RESPONSE

A full consideration of all the ways God wants us to repel the World, the Flesh and the Devil is beyond the scope of this book[a]. In brief, the general response is:

- Reject the passions and desires of the flesh as providing only fleeting and hollow pleasure, destructive of how and for what God made you (Galatians 5.24)
- Reject the World's deceptive plans for our happiness and embrace God's (Ephesians 1.3-14)

---

[a] See *Made to Be Like Him*.

- Put on the whole armor of God against the wiles of the Devil . . . through faith, the Word of God, and prayer (Ephesians 6). Translation: constantly remember God's love for us and our salvation in Christ.

The bigger picture is to embrace fully God's plan for our life. The key to embracing God's plan on a daily basis? Calling on God's power, which we will consider next.

Application Question #3 – Describe where you have personally observed the Evil One at work or where you believe his hand is at work in society.

_____

_____

_____

Fear Not!

Are not five sparrows sold for two pennies? And not one of them is forgotten before God. Why, even the hairs of your head are all numbered. Fear not; you are of more value than many sparrows . . . Fear not, little flock, for it is your Father's good pleasure to give you the kingdom.

Luke 12.6-7,32

---

3 – Tapping God's Power

St. Peter's Basilica, Bernini

Rekindle the gift of God that is within you through the laying on of hands [baptism and confirmation] . . . a spirit of power and love and self control.

I Timothy 1.6-7

Christianity is no self-improvement program! It's a letting-God-transform-me-by-His-Power program. You don't pay for it with bucks (at least directly). We pay for it by laying down our life, taking up our cross and taking Jesus as our Lord. The improvements are eternal not ephemeral. Rather than growing self-confident, we grow into the stature required to be an intimate friend of the most powerful, awe-inspiring being in the universe. Rather than gaining wealth, we become heirs to the Kingdom of Everything. Rather than learning how to win friends and influence people, a radiance of love, joy and humility proves irresistible to those around us. Rather than supercharging our career, physique, and love life – whatever – we prepare ourselves for an eternity of joy.

When you think about it, the promises of Christianity do boggle the mind – the promises of becoming like Christ are so outrageous that advertising them probably should be outlawed! We're supposed to look like Christ, the image of the invisible God, as it says in Colossians 1? Despite the world, the flesh and the Devil? In reality, these claims are all so much hot air unless you tap into the Holy Spirit, "who restores the baptized to the divine likeness lost through sin" and "makes us act out of love"[a].

THE POWER PLANT

Consider how the following passages apply to your life; how can you respond practically to the following Scripture passages?

---

[a] CCC 734 and 1972, respectively.

Ephesians 1.19 & 3.20

_____

_____

_____

Galatians 2.20

_____

_____

_____

II Corinthians 12.9-10

_____

_____

_____

> ### The Law of Grace: Acting out of love infused by the Holy Spirit?
>
> The New Testament moral teaching requires "virtues that flow from faith in Christ and are animated by charity, the principal gift of the Holy Spirit. " (CCC 1971) "The New Law is called a *law of love* because it makes us act out of the love infused by the Holy Spirit, rather than from fear; a *law of grace*, because it confers the strength of grace to act, by means of faith and the sacraments; a *law of freedom*, because it sets us free from the ritual and juridical observances of the Old Law, inclines us to act spontaneously by the prompting of charity."   (CCC 1972)

John 15.4-5

_____

_____

Now we are asking the big questions! So how do we *abide* with Jesus? You may be able to guess the answer. In John we see Jesus identify the Eucharist as a way of abiding in him (John 6.56). Take another look at the quote opening this chapter. John also speaks about this power in John 7.37-39. What is another way of tapping into God's power?

_____

_____

_____

SPIRITUALLY CONNECTED

> *How can the Holy Spirit be our life if our heart is far from him?*
>
> CCC 2744

We access God's power – the gift of the Holy Spirit – by asking for it. Grace is God's power to make us holy and to use us in evangelism and to help the Church grow[a]. and is a gift of the Holy Spirit Like the Samaritan women who lived in a dry land and had to fetch water every day for their survival, we need to drink of the Holy Spirit *daily* if not *hourly* to survive and flourish (see John 4 and 7.37-39).

---

[a] CCC 2003. Grace has other important dimensions including justification. See CCC 1996-2029. This study will refer to grace primarily in terms of God's power and simply as (the work of) the Holy Spirit.

We access God's power through our regular daily prayer time as well as through the sacraments of the Church; for good reason is the Church called the Temple of the Holy Spirit. We power our electrical appliances by continuously connecting to the electrical utility. Similarly, God powers lives of holiness and love by the Holy Spirit.

Prayer is how we connect to God's power grid. Fasting can amp up prayer[a]. Stay connected throughout the day by praying constantly. Make staying connected to God a higher priority than staying connected to news, family, friends, and work associates through cell phones, email and the web. Make your prayers very specific.

> ***Cardinal Suenens on Toasters***
>
> Cardinal Suenen, one of the architects of Vatican II, once said that the Christian life is like a toaster: it doesn't work unless you plug it in. You plug it in by receiving the Holy Spirit.

TOP THREE DAILY PRIORITIES

What were yesterday's top three priorities?

1. _____

2. _____

3. _____

What were last weekend's top three priorities?

1. _____

2. _____

3. _____

Now, consider, if God is going to transform us, we had better stay close to God! In fact, staying connected to God and his people is the one absolutely necessary condition for God to work in our lives. We connect with God through developing a **life of daily prayer and through celebrating the Eucharist**. A life of daily prayer is based upon listening to God, preeminently through Sacred Scripture, and feasting on his goodness, truth and beauty. In his presence we will be transformed; away from God, all efforts at becoming like Jesus are futile. By design, God's plan succeeds only by actively connecting to him through a prayer and sacramental life. Make no

---

[a] See Matthew 6.16-18 and CCC 2549.

mistake: American culture assaults you daily with its plans and programs for just about every minute of our life. If we fail to make daily prayer the absolute top priority in our life, we will quickly fade into the woodwork of our godless and materialistic society, or, at best, maintain a threadbare relationship with God until some shock eventually severs it completely. Review the discussion of prayer in Part I, chapters 4-6.

Just to be safe, better make daily prayer not just our top priority, but numbers two and three as well!

Application Questions

1. What needs to change in your life for your prayer and sacramental life to become your top priorities?

> #### Prayer - God Commands It?
>
> Just in case the Thessalonians thought he was merely dispensing *good advice*, St. Paul stresses that one of the core teachings throughout his writings is a matter of obeying *God's explicit commands*. Read Ephesians 6.18 (cf. CCC 2742-3). What is God's will for you in Christ Jesus?
>
> _____
> _____
> _____

_____
_____
_____
_____
_____

2. Do you find it challenging to ask for God's help all the time? Why or why not? What might help?

_____
_____
_____
_____
_____

LIFETIME QUEST? DEALING WITH LEGACY SIN

While daily or hourly prayer fuels our transformation, how many days or years will it take? When we become saints? The answer ultimately depends on how fully we give ourselves over to God's plan for our life, and to some degree, on overcoming the residual damage of our sin and those of others.

As society veers further from God's plans, unless we were still more deliberate and energetic in pursuing God's plan, our lives likely reflect damage from the "world" – which often can be rather ugly. For example, something like half of those counting themselves Christian men in the U.S. have serious pornography, masturbation or other sexual addictions. Many of us are scarred emotionally from divorce or abuse. Extramarital sex and broken relationships may seriously undermine our ability to form permanent marital relationships or trust our spouses; like society, we come to view our partner mainly through sexual eyes. Society's intense pre-occupation with physical, academic and professional achievement may deeply distort one's self image. Enslavery to greed, pride, and fear encloses us in ourselves, isolating us from God and other people and damaging those around us. Craving love and attention from fellow human beings who are themselves increasingly self-absorbed contributes to a variety of emotional illnesses, such as eating disorders. Dysfunctional and disordered families and the world's hyper-emphasis on sexual fulfillment – in addition to the above factors – help fuel same-sex attractions.

Sin and wounded-ness do have a way of multiplying in a person's life. In fact, sin can "infect" or exacerbate any pre-existing wounded-ness. In a society that glorifies vice and sneers at God's plans, the multiplication and corresponding damage is often exponential. The ways in which we have been damaged by our own sins and shortcomings – and by those of others – can be called "legacy sin". One definition of legacy is:

Something handed down from an ancestor or a predecessor or from the past.[a]

In the case of legacy sin, what is handed down is from our own "past" involving our own or others sins and shortcomings. For example, there may be a pattern of criticism which our parents picked up from, and were subjected to by, our grandparents and perhaps even our great grandparents. When we in turn grow up in a home permeated by criticism we are both wounded by that criticism and often begin to practice it ourselves. Thus before we can come to experience God's love, we may need to be healed from that wound and sin of criticism. Some of our parents lacked—to varying degrees—the ability to love us well, to provide for our emotional and spiritual needs. This deficit produces deep wounds, especially in infants and young children. These wounds in turn, can affect our capacity both to experience God's love and to live out what He commands.

But we need not remain stuck in our wounded-ness and patterns of sin. For Christ came precisely to "preach the Good News to the poor"—which is especially those of us who are weak, wounded, addicted, emotionally distressed, etc. Furthermore, he said "I have come to heal sinners, not the virtuous." As He draws us to Himself, we may see that we need help from others in addressing the wounds and sins of our past or present (such as addiction). God has provided us with many resources to address these problems, including qualified psychologists and other professionals, the sacrament of confession and spiritual direction. A variety of programs and ministries provide specific and general help in healing such as Marriage Encounter, Retrouvaille, twelve step programs (e.g., AA), etc. Please see www.GodsPlanforYourLife.org for a listing of some of these programs.

---

[a] *The American Heritage® Dictionary of the English Language*, Fourth Edition, downloaded from Dictionary.com on June 11, 2005.

Perhaps the most healing reality of all is the Body of Christ—those fellow Christians who are emotionally healthy and can nurture and love us into being the person God intended us to be. Spend time with loving people transformed by Christ and you will begin to experience the love of God which is the most powerful healer of all.

4 – Fighting the Good Fight: Our Effort

Work out your own salvation with fear and trembling;
for God is at work in you, both to will and to work for his good pleasure.

Not that I have already obtained this or am already perfect; but I press on . . .
forgetting what lies behind and straining forward to what lies ahead, I press on
toward the goal for the prize of the upward call of God in Christ Jesus.

Philippians 2.12-13; 3.12-14

It is true that God forgives us and makes us holy and charitable *by his power*, but only to the extent we ask his forgiveness and join our will to his. This *joining our will to his* is where the rub comes in. We may be convinced that our highest joy and happiness is found precisely in becoming like Christ and loving others, but the process of such transformation and living a life of charity may be hard, at least at first, and always costly. Look at our master: Jesus came to serve others at the cost of strenuous daily effort and ultimately supreme humiliation and pain. Like our master, embracing the Father's will for us requires strenuous daily effort, although only a few of us will ever be called to anything like our Lord's sacrifice. All of us must contend with a world generally hostile to God's plan, together with overcoming our own sinful tendencies and our spiritual enemies, as discussed in Chapter 2. However sweet the reward, following the Lord implies taking up our cross and the attitude of a servant – and this takes effort on our part.

Discipleship starts with making Jesus lord of our lives and putting everything aside to follow him, as discussed in Part I, Chapter 3. Living out his lordship requires three things:

1) Awareness of God's Will
2) God's power
3) Our effort

The Spirit of God through Scripture and the Church makes us aware of God's will for us. Chapters 5-10 of this book consider God's will according to three general elements: being with him and his people, becoming like him and loving whom he loves, in other words, to conversion, transformation and mission. God further provides the power – grace – to be transformed in holiness and charity and to live out our respective missions, as discussed in the last chapter. It is up to us to join our efforts[a] to his power in living our lives as "new creations", which we will explore further in this chapter.

---

[a] Although, somewhat paradoxically, such effort on our part is itself only possible because God so inclines us, CCC 2001.

BLESSED ARE THOSE WHO . . . *SHOW EFFORT*

I have fought the good fight . . . there is reserved for me the crown of righteousness.

II Timothy 4

Blessed are those who hunger and thirst, are persecuted, mourn, make peace . . . think about it: the beatitudes all require effort. As much as the New Testament proclaims God's power at work in us, it also greatly emphasizes the need for our effort: faith without works is dead (James 2). As we considered in Chapter 3 of Part I, Jesus graphically and personally, as it were, measures the effort required to follow him in terms of taking up a cross of crucifixion on a daily basis. Analogies of striving, conflict, building, war and even self mutilation[a] nail home the effort Jesus expects of us in loving others, from "washing feet" to laying down our lives. The effort is even more radical when we consider how Jesus expands the circle of people whom we are to serve beyond our friends and family (although loving those closest to us can be the greatest challenge!).

Read Luke 10.29-37 and Matthew 5.43-47. Who are the "others" whom we are to love and serve?

_____

_____

_____

Paul translates taking up our cross into the supreme effort of "crucifying our flesh with its passions and desires" and our servant-hood as pointing to becoming slaves of one another in love. Paul repeatedly uses the language of soldiering to describe the perseverance and intensity of battle in the Christian life[b]. Consider Paul's instruction on effort to one of his key disciples in II Timothy 2.1-5. What metaphors does Paul use in describing the effort he expects from Timothy?

_____

_____

_____

Being a disciple is not for sissies. In fact, one of the lessons from the Sermon on the Mount in Matthew 5-7 is that no amount of effort on our part will bring us to the perfection of holiness and charity that God requires: being Jesus' disciple is impossible without his power. Yet the Lord expects us to throw everything we've got into this business.

---

[a] Luke 13.24, Luke 12.51-53, Luke 14.28-31, and Matthew 5.29-30. Cf. Luke 18.9.
[b] E.g., Galatians 5.13, 24; Ephesians 6.10-17.

FOCUS OF OUR EFFORTS

Put to death the deeds of the body . . .
Put on the Lord Jesus Christ   Romans 8.13; 13.14

The focus of our efforts to grow as disciples include the following:

1) eliminating sins (vices) and fighting temptations (spiritual warfare)
2) developing habits of being good and loving others (virtues and the fruit of the Spirit)
3) seeking out and embracing God's specific plan for our daily lives

Yet it would be wrong to say that our goals are simply moral improvement and obedience to God. Rather, we are striving to put on Jesus Christ, walk by the Spirit, partake in the divine nature, and receive God's very own Spirit and power for holiness. We have all met "morally correct" people who are lifeless and flat, doing the right things but without warmth or love. Far more alive are people into whose hearts God has poured his very own Spirit, far warmer are those basking in the glow of the Father's tremendous love, utterly irresistible are those whose faces have grown radiant with the beauty and glory of the living God. Indeed, the focus of our efforts transcends (and fulfills) all morality: it is to collaborate in God's work of truly becoming "new creations" after the image of his own son.

The first two of these categories relate to growth in holiness and Christian character and, following the above quote from Romans 8, involve "putting to death the deeds of the body" and "putting on Jesus Christ"[a]. The final category of effort – embracing God's plan for our daily lives - is really quite broad but the following elements apply to everyone:

- Prayer and Sacramental Life
- Christian Identity and Worldview
- Loving and Caring for others
- Christian Pattern of Life
- Strong Family Life
- Christian Fellowship
- Life of Mission

Saving further exploration of these elements until later chapters, the next section considers some of the ways in which we can collaborate with God's work. What types of effort can we make in striving for this transformation? We know the Lord requires maximum effort on our part – what does this look like on a practical basis?

---

[a] Cf. the terminology of Colossians 3: "putting to death what is earthly in us" and "putting on our new nature".

TYPES OF EFFORT

Be Serious and Discipline Yourselves   I Peter 4.7

We have already considered in Part I, Chapter 3 the effort of laying down our lives and giving them to Christ. This process of dying to ourselves is often one that we must revisit again and again in our Christian lives. It's as if our old flesh has nine *thousand* lives! This act of faith in a small way resembles Jesus' effort in the garden just before his arrest: not my will, but yours be done. The Church in her pastoral wisdom invites us to repeat our baptismal vows once or twice during the liturgical year partly in order to re-affirm Jesus' lordship over our lives, the counter-part of which is dying to our self. In a certain way, we draw down from the treasury of Jesus' effort of laying down his life every time we receive communion inasmuch as we participate in his salvific act.

Sometimes our effort is simply to "let go" of our lives. We can so easily clench our lives like a fist grasping money that God must wrench it free with great force (with our permission, of course). This wrenching could take the form of literally losing someone or something very dear to us, such as a job, spouse, parent, child, our health, an honor, etc. For some of us, our "effort" may involve our will being broken, in the manner of a trainer breaking in a young horse. The effort is mostly on the part of the trainer; the horse at some point just "lets go of his will". Perhaps our effort in laying down our lives involved the pain of wrenching or of being broken.

Application Question. Describe the effort required in making Jesus Lord of your life.

_____

_____

_____

_____

Don't be surprised if there comes a point where you find yourself back on the throne of your life and need to repeat this process. Or perhaps you are in that position now. If so, the best thing to do is to let go of your life (to avoid the pain, if for no other reason) and give your whole life to God, right now, without reservation. Simply pray,

> Oh God, I give my life fully to you without reservation: I am yours. Be lord of my life.
> Take me, hold me, do with me as you see fit.
> In the name of the Father and of the Son and of the Holy Spirit, Amen.

The exertion of giving your life to God, itself made possible by his grace, may be your greatest and creates the foundation for discipleship, including the elements described above, which will be further considered in Chapters 5-10. What efforts are helpful for growing as a disciple? The following chart lists some efforts and associated aspects of discipleship.

TYPE OF EFFORT	PRAYER AND SACRAMENTAL LIFE	CHRISTIAN IDENTITY & WORLDVIEW	HOLINESS & CHRISTIAN CHARACTER – Put to Death Sin	– Put on Christ	– Maintenance & Growth	CHRISTIAN PATTERN OF LIFE	LOVING & CARING FOR OTHERS	STRONG FAMILY LIFE	CHRISTIAN FELLOWSHIP	LIFE OF MISSION
CONVERSION										
fear eternal separation from Father (imperfect contrition)			+							
mourn over our sins and vices			+							
avoid the near occasion of sin			+		+	+		+		
hate evil and sin		+	+	+						
hunger for righteousness		+	+	+	+					+
SACRAMENTAL & DEVOTIONAL										
PRAYER AND EUCHARIST (daily)	+	+	+	+	+	+	+	+	+	+
CONFESSION	+		+	+	+	+		+		
fear offending the Father (perfect contrition)		+	+	+	+					
do penance and make reparation			+							
EXAMINE CONSCIENCE (DAILY)	+	+	+	+	+	+	+	+	+	+
perform spiritual warfare	+	+	+	+	+			+	+	+
take Lent as a season of prayer, fasting and almsgiving	+	+	+	+	+	+	+	+		+
fast (weekly)			+	+	+	+		+		+
spiritual reading (weekly if not daily)		+	+	+	+	+	+	+		+
GROWTH AND TRANSFORMATION										
exercise self-discipline & self-control	+		+	+	+	+	+	+	+	+
be accountable to, and encouraged by, a faith sharing group	+	+	+	+	+	+	+	+	+	+
be pure of heart	+	+	+	+	+		+	+	+	+
be poor in spirit: simplicity of life	+	+	+	+	+	+	+	+	+	+
be meek: rely on God for our power		+	+	+	+	+	+	+		+
be humble: see yourself as you are	+	+	+	+	+	+		+	+	+
focus effort on one virtue or fruit of the Spirit at a time				+	+					
"train" in the face of adversity and hardship				+	+		+	+	+	+
be committed & persevere: we are "in it for the long haul"	+		+	+	+		+	+	+	+
become "slaves" to one another in love				+	+	+	+	+	+	+
spend ourselves for the kingdom: apostolic suffering				+	+	+		+		+

We know that prayer and the Eucharist are the foundation of our efforts, being most helpful for all aspects of discipleship. Our prayer life, considered in Part I of this book, has a pivotal role in our transformation: we must constantly ask for God's help. Accessing God's power for change through prayer, confession and the Eucharist cannot be emphasized enough. Some of the types of efforts are really virtues or character traits, which are more precisely habits or dispositions to act. Much could be said about all of these types of efforts, which is one of the topics of *Made to Be Like Him*.

Daily Examination of Conscience

Examine yourselves to see whether you are living in the faith, test yourselves.

II Corinthians 13.5

A daily examination of conscience is how we measure our efforts in embracing God's plan for our life (among other things). We first form our consciences according to God's law as found in Scripture and Church teaching. Since Jesus is lord of our lives, we must sensitize our consciences to the *imperatives of discipleship*: becoming like Jesus and loving whom God loves – which imperatives, in fact, this book tries to help you apply concretely to your life. A daily examination of conscience considers the following:

- Love of God and Neighbor ("life of charity")
- Sin ("violations of holiness")
- Discipleship Effort

God is going to do everything he can on his part to draw us, woo us, charm us, guide us, shock us and even frighten us into accepting the magnificent life he has planned out for us, but we have to say yes and seek after him with all our hearts. God provides the power to become holy and loving, yet it takes real effort to take up this new life. Next to daily prayer and the sacraments, examining ourselves every day is the most important discipline for spiritual growth. St. Ignatius, in fact, recommends examining our consciences *twice each day*! So, how do we do it? I recommend the following guidelines[a].

At first, make sure you have properly formed your conscience as to **violations of holiness**, i.e., what offends our all-holy God. Depending on your catechetical background and how much your conscience has been shaped by the world and dulled by patterns of sin, this may take some time. The most complete guide is the *Catechism*, especially the section on the Ten Commandments (paragraphs 2052-2557) and its index. Chapter 6 briefly discusses the life of holiness. The examination of conscience in the appendix is a handy reference yet contains only a partial listing of sins. Our response to violations of holiness is repentance, asking God's forgiveness, and, perhaps, making reparation and doing penance. Major violations (grave or mortal sin) also *require* reconciliation through the sacrament of confession. Confession is also *very helpful* in overcoming minor violations (venial sin) and *may be necessary* inasmuch as venial sins harden into habits and can eventually kill off your life with God.

The **life of charity** is a life of loving others expressed by tangibly caring for those around you, starting with God and your families. The mark of charity towards God is joy, manifested in a continuous and relatively passive manner as cheerfulness and a fundamental disposition of

---

[a] Many important things touched on here, such as conscience, contrition and mortal sin, which warrant further development such as can be found in the Catechism. *Made to be Like Him* also provides a more extensive treatment of these concepts.

gratitude and awe. Are we actively loving God by obeying him, spending time with him in prayer, and loving others? The mark of charity towards others is patience, gentleness, esteem, and even tenderness. Charity towards neighbor must be expressed in practical and concrete ways. Remember, we can't love God who we can't see if we fail to love those around us whom we can see and that faith without works is dead, according to Saints John and James.

Are you really trying? The chart above will help you measure your **discipleship effort.** In a certain way, the daily examination of conscience is the parent of all discipleship effort, both as a means of nurturing and of disciplining other efforts.

Don't wait to begin a daily examination of conscience until you've got a perfectly formed conscience: start today with what you've got and build from there! I suggest performing your examination in the evening just before bed and keeping it brief, say, three to five minutes, although you may initially and on occasion find spending more time helpful. Remind yourself in the morning of anything that deserves further prayer. Limit your review to the last day and develop a set of examination questions that fit your challenges with sin, the life of charity and discipleship effort as well as particular areas of growth such as establishing a prayer time or acquiring a particular virtue. Keep your daily examination simple and doable; we needn't be as exhaustive as in preparing for confession.

APPLICATION EXERCISE

To get started, develop your own daily examination of conscience by completing the chart below. Consult the Examination of Conscience for Daily Use in the For Further Study Section to help fill out some questions particular to you in each area.

I. Loving God with all our heart, mind and soul
- Have I prayed, read Scripture or went to Mass today?
- Was my demeanor one of joy, cheerfulness, and gratitude?
- _____
- _____
- _____

II. Loving our neighbor as our self
- Did I cheerful serve my family, those for whom I am responsible, and my neighbor?
- Have I interceded for those who don't know Christ?
- Was I humble, kind, generous, chaste, and patient with others?
- How did I fail to love others as Christ would have?
- _____
- _____
- _____

III. Keeping the Commandments

- Did I "idolize" some material possession, worldly or spiritual fame, or someone's affection?
- Did I say the Lord's name in anger or carelessly?
- Did I go to Sunday Mass? Did I work needlessly on Sunday?
- _____
- Did I properly care for my parents?
- _____
- Did I harm or sin against anybody?
- _____
- Did I fail to be chaste, i.e., to avoid any form of lust?
- _____
- Was I completely fair in my work and dealings with others?
- _____
- Was I completely honest with everyone?
- _____
- Did I give reign to thoughts of wishing I was married to another person?
- Did I grow frustrated or despair because I am not married?
- _____
- Have I been materialistic or pre-occupied with acquiring something?
- _____

IV. Keeping Church Law

- Have I supported the Church?
- Have I been reverential at Mass, especially by observing the communion fast?
- _____

You can access other examination of conscience templates at www.GodsPlanForYourLife.org.

Becoming Like Jesus (*Transformation*)

Michelangelo, Sistine Chapel

5 - Being Changed from One Degree of Glory to the Next

As we saw in Part I, we gain true and eternal joy from experiencing God's love as well as beholding Him who is ablaze with a love, holiness and beauty beyond our imagining, both now through prayer and in heaven when we see him face to face. You are made for this joy.

As we draw near to God, he transforms us into his own likeness. The Holy Spirit not only makes us look like him and act like him, but comes to motivate and animate our desires. Chief among these desires are longing simply to be with God and His people and a certain profound pleasure in loving others. Counter-cultural, eh?

> We all, with unveiled face, beholding the glory of the Lord, are being changed into his likeness from one degree of glory to another; for this comes from the Lord who is the Spirit. . . . Therefore, if any one is in Christ, he is a new creation; the old has passed away, behold, the new has come.
>
> II Corinthians 3:18, 5.17

The key ingredient for this transformation on our side, as with gaining a relationship with God and growing in prayer, is that we must ask for it. We must *ask God* to change us – I should say, *get in the habit of asking God* to change us as it's probably going to take a while! Of course, we also struggle to embrace God's work by deliberating focusing our will, avoiding occasions of sin, practicing virtue whether we enjoy it or not, and generally, as St. Paul says, by *running the race* and *fighting the good fight* until we reach heaven.

THE JERK PROBLEM

As we saw earlier in Part I, change is not optional: we must become perfect as our heavenly father is perfect, holy as he is holy, loving as he is loving. It all sounds a little circular. Basically, God doesn't want to be surrounded by jerks. You and I, to modify a phrase from Alcoholics Anonymous, are *recovering jerks*, more or less (I speak here with much personal authority). Forgiven jerks, but still wanting to do jerky things. So God is going to make us wonderful people both for our sake and his sake (and our collective sakes), because we are going to be with him forever, right?

> Sanctifying grace . . . perfects the soul itself *to enable it to live with God, to act by his love.*   CCC 2000

Why prolong your misery? For all of our sakes, start asking God to change you! These next few chapters are mainly about translating "your asking" into tangible concrete steps. Actually, this chapter is something of a teaser because the steps to becoming like Christ require another short book if not our lifetime. The next chapter merely lays out the big picture of how God transforms us and considers some first steps. The concluding chapters consider some practical aspects of loving whom God loves – and loving it!

Describe some areas of your life that you wish God to transform:

1. _____

2. _____

3. _____

THE BIG PICTURE: BECOMING NEW CREATIONS

Something needs to happen in order for us to behold God himself, even beyond Jesus forgiving our sins! We actually become new creations by . . . dying and rising with Jesus through our Baptism. Consider the following passage:

> You were buried with him in Baptism, in which you were also raised with him through faith in the working of God, who raised him from the dead. And you, who were dead in trespasses and the un-circumcision of your flesh, **God made alive together with him**, having forgiven us all our trespasses, having canceled the bond which stood against us with its legal demands; this he set aside, nailing it to the cross. If then you have been **raised with Christ**, seek the things that are above, where Christ is, seated at the right hand of God. **Put to death** therefore what is earthly in you: fornication, impurity, passion, evil desire, and covetousness, which is idolatry . . . **put on the new nature**, which is being renewed in knowledge after the image of its creator.
>
> Colossians 2:12-14; 3:1,5,10

Didn't know Paul bolded stuff, did you? Put in your own words what Paul says happens to us through Baptism here and in Romans 6.3-11:

_____

_____

_____

_____

_____

How does Paul's "point of view" change in II Corinthians 5:16-17? How would you describe his new perspective mean?

_____

_____

_____

_____

_____

God's plan for us really defies comprehension. God wants to make us not just any "new creation" or give us just any "new nature" but the very likeness of Jesus himself:

> Those who love him, who are called according to his purpose . . . he also predestined to be conformed to the image of his Son, in order that he might be the first-born among many brethren.
> Romans 8.28-9

It is in Christ, "the image of the invisible God," that man has been created "in the image and likeness" of the Creator. It is in Christ, Redeemer and Savior, that the divine image, disfigured in man by the first sin, has been restored to its original beauty and ennobled by the grace of God.   CCC 1701

SO JUST WHAT ARE WE GOING TO LOOK LIKE?

Yeah, yeah – you got it, right? We're going to look like Jesus sooner or later, at least if we plan on being with God in heaven. What does "being conformed to the image of Jesus" mean exactly? To get started, it may help to consider the "best of the best" human beings you've encountered, then we'll move on to the Saints and Jesus himself. Think of some of the people over the course of your life that you loved most or most enjoyed being with and list them together with what you like most about them:

Favorite People   Prized Traits or Deeds

1. _____   • _____
                                                          • _____
                                                          • _____

2. _____   • _____
                                                          • _____
                                                          • _____

3. _____   • _____
                                                          • _____
                                                          • _____

This exercise helps us begin to imagine what incredible beings God intends to make us. You probably know some pretty wonderful people, which gives us a mere hint of the wonderful creatures God intends to makes us. Yet, unless you happen to be living amongst fully transformed saints, our holiness and virtue will far surpass the best of what we've seen or experienced of our family, friends and acquaintances.

The Church does hold up for our imitation and instruction certain men and women overflowing with the power of God's grace, renowned for personal holiness and love of God: canonized saints. Take the docility of Mary, the Mother of God, who through incredible faith accepts the apparent mark of an extramarital affair that often resulted in being stoned to death. Considering the lives of those already changed to a large degree into Jesus' likeness gives us a pretty good idea of what we will look like when God's done with us. Read books on the lives of various saints – and imitate them!

Saints are the most beautiful and fascinating of people. Rather than starchy, prudish and self-satisfied, saints are wonderful and joyful. After all, they have been changed into the image of the One who radiates love, beauty, joy, and goodness. So now you have the answer as to why eternal joy comes from being with God's people as well as with God himself.

What was Jesus really like? What kind of man was he? Fortunately, the Gospels paint a pretty good portrait. Describe some of Jesus' qualities depicted in John 11.1-42:

_____

_____

_____

_____

Reasoning again by analogy, consider any virtue and the person who best exemplifies it: comparing their virtue to Jesus' is like comparing a candle to the sun. Indeed, it would be foolish to compare the love, joy, peace, patience, kindness, goodness, faithfulness, gentleness and self control of Jesus with the virtue of any other person. God's love, for starters, is incomparably richer and more tangible than that of any human being. How can God really love me with all my foibles and follies, all my sins and sadness? Look at my history – who could know every moment of my existence and still look upon me with love? With a love so intense that he desires me with him forever, as a friend?

I suggest reading through one of the gospels in one sitting, perhaps Luke (which might take an hour), while asking Jesus to reveal himself more deeply to you. Look particularly for individual encounters Jesus has with various people. You will be amazed at the largeness of God's personality and the richness of his voice speaking to you.

The Best of Men (but then I'm biased)

The morning Dad died I was standing around the kitchen with the priest who was Dad's spiritual director. With a surprising twinkle in his eye, he said, "you know, your father told me it was the best year of his life" (Dad's illness lasted about a year). Just what I had been thinking. And at the funeral Mom said it was hers! Are we a morose lot? Actually, no.

For a guy successful at whatever he put his hand to and full of good friends, a year of struggling with cancer shouldn't be your best. That year did turn Dad from being generally affable and self-contented though sometimes irascible to deeply loving and appreciative, reliable in his tenderness and concern for us. Never, unless you really pried, would he mention the constant discomfort and finally terrible pain from the cancer. In the midst of extreme nausea, for example, he would greet my wife very tenderly and compliment her nice outfit.

Our family saw God transform Dad from a pretty good man into an ideal father and husband, full of fatherly wisdom, holiness and care for others – and funnier than ever. I hope to spend eternity with Dad and people like him.

APPLICATION QUESTIONS

1. How does God make us better persons?

    _____

    _____

    _____

    _____

    _____

2. What is our role in God making us better persons?

    _____

    _____

    _____

    _____

    _____

The Ultimate Perfume

Through saints, God spreads in every place the fragrance that comes from knowing him
. . . the aroma of Christ.   II Corinthians 2.14-15

---

6 - Holiness, Personal Identity & World View

> His divine power has granted to us all things that pertain to life and godliness, through the knowledge of him who called us *to his own glory and excellence,* by which he has granted to us his precious and very great promises, that through these you may escape from the corruption that is in the world because of passion, and *become partakers of the divine nature.* I Peter 1.3-4

The last chapter considered our glorious call to be sons and daughters of God, to be new creations in Christ that resemble God himself, even, as we see in the above quote, to be partakers in the divine nature! OK, so what does this mean, exactly? God wants to transform all aspects of our lives – our morality and character, our identity, our view of the world, our use of time and resources, those with whom we spend time, and the very pattern of our daily lives[a]. This chapter considers God's plan for us:

1. to be holy by transforming our morality and character;
2. to take our identity as his children; members of his body; temples of the Holy Spirit; stewards; and missionaries.
3. to see the "world" as he sees it

Chapters 7 and 8 will consider other practical aspects of how God wishes to transform our lives. The final chapters then consider God's plan for us to embrace mission

HOLINESS: MORALITY & CHARACTER

Conversion leads us to life with God and his people. In Baptism, the connection to life with God is instantaneous. If our faith is re-awakened as an adult, repentance and receiving the sacrament of reconciliation immediately re-establishes our life with God and his people. Yet, especially in American society, our lives don't automatically reflect our conversion.

Take a moment and honestly consider the areas of Christian morality with which you struggle (don't worry, you won't be forced to share this if you are working through this book in a small group). In what areas do you struggle most on a daily basis?

_____

---

[a] Here again, I note the inadequacies of space and refer you to the planned companion to this book, *Made to Be Like Him*; check www.GodsPlanforYourLife.org for further details, and in the mean time, consult the Life in Christ section of the CCC, 1691-2558 and your local Catholic bookstore. You will find a decent amount of material in the CCC by simply checking the topical index at the back of the book.

_____

_____

_____

Morality and character are interrelated: morality and its embedded values inform us what to do and avoid doing; character is how consistently one lives out a given morality. Osama bin Laden might have terrific character, but screwed up values and morality. Jesus sums up *what to do* as "loving God with all your heart, mind and soul and loving your neighbor as yourself". He also emphatically endorses the Law of Moses for what *not to do*, even making compliance a condition for being with God[a].

After we undergo conversion, our **character** often retains a form based on our former morality or way of living ("living according to the flesh"). All our moral habits make up our character. A habit is moral if it involves doing right or wrong. Possessing honesty is being in the habit of telling the truth. Our moral choices and habits help determine who we are; we slowly become what we choose. Telling lies soon changes you into a liar. One retains the habit of lying even when you want to tell the truth. God needs to transform all of these negative moral habits – vices – into their opposite as well as create all kinds of good moral habits – virtues – that reflect our new identity as sons and daughters of God, after the pattern of Jesus. The Lord himself discusses character throughout the Sermon on the Mount in Matthew 5-7. Paul discusses the Christian moral life in Romans 12-15; I Corinthians 12-13; Colossians 3-4; Ephesians 4-5, and elsewhere. Paul lists the fruit of the Spirit in Galatians 5[b].

As the Holy Spirit dwells in us, the **fruit of the Spirit** becomes abundant in our lives: love, joy, peace, patience, kindness, goodness, faithfulness and self-control[c].

Which fruit of the Spirit do you wish to flourish more in your life?

_____

_____

Do you struggle with whether God's morality is best for you – *its truth*? For example, are you convinced that there is harm in viewing pornography? Or that loving our enemy – even terrorists – is really the right thing to do? Why?

_____

_____

_____

---

[a] Matthew 5.17-20, which, as we have seen, drives us to God himself on a daily – if not hourly - basis, in order to gain the power to do so: his Holy Spirit. The *Catechism of the Catholic Church* systematically lays out the Lord's teaching on morality in 2052 to 2558, following the order implied by the Ten Commandments.
[b] Ibid.
[c] Galatians 5.22-23.

As God is holy, so also must we **become holy.** More than simply "pretty good", God intends for our character to become God-like! God is the source of all goodness; he is pure goodness. Jesus is the measure of perfect righteousness and perfect love. Taking Jesus' character doesn't render dry, rule-following persons striving to do one good deed after another. Rather, God transforms and sets our hearts afire for all that is good, true and beautiful and against all that is evil, false and deformed. All of our passions and appetites come to resemble God's: being and doing "good", even at great personal cost, becomes almost irresistible.

PERSONAL IDENTITY AS GOD'S CHILDREN, MEMBERS OF HIS BODY & TEMPLES OF THE HOLY SPIRIT

You have received the spirit of sonship. When we cry, "Abba! Father!"
it is the Spirit himself bearing witness with our spirit that we are children of God,
and if children, then heirs, heirs of God and fellow heirs with Christ, provided we suffer with him
in order that we may also be glorified with him.

Romans 8.15-17

How do you think of yourself? What labels or adjectives best describe you, e.g., plumber, student, homemaker, doctor, an American, attractive, funny, Irish, single, son of God, etc.? Just list off what comes to mind without asking how *you should* think of yourself.

1. _____

2. _____

3. _____

4. _____

5. _____

Our deepest identity should be based on God's unwavering love for us. He knows *you* intimately. He shaped *you* in your mother's womb, knows when *you* sit and when *you* stand, he knows all *your* thoughts, what *you* are going to say before *you* say it, he even has a detailed plan for *your* life (Psalm 139). He loves *you* so incredibly much that he sent his son to make amends for our wrongdoing. He loves us so much that he adopts us as children. Like a good parent, he is completely on our side, he is utterly for us and nothing can separate us from his paternal love (Romans 8.15-39). God's love even has a maternal dimension, comparable to a hen protectively gathering together her chicks (Luke 13.34). Our fundamental identity as God's children is fully secure by God's unwavering love.

Do you not know that your bodies are members of Christ?
Do you not know that your body is a temple of the Holy Spirit within you,
which you have from God?

I Corinthians 6.15,19

Do we think of ourselves as members of Jesus' body? This identity has both a vertical and horizontal dimension. Vertically, we are organically connected to God, but horizontally to each other. This organic connection is developed throughout I Corinthians and is a major theme of the New Testament. God himself in the person of the Holy Spirit indwells this body. Actually, Scripture refers to indwelling us as individual persons but also as the collection of all believers. The intimacy God intends to have with us is so intense, so dazzling that our language literally fails.

Do we think of ourselves as God does? God sees a person in whom his Spirit dwells, one with whom he is intimately present. God sees us as men and women knit together closely in community, as members of his body, the Church. That is how God sees us.

To become like Jesus we also must think like God, particularly in terms of how we see ourselves. Little does God see and value athletic prowess, intellectual gifts, physical beauty, social attractiveness, or station in life. Rather, in whoever accepts his gift of new life God sees his son or daughter, a member of his household, and one clothed with the dignity of Jesus and filled with his own Spirit.

PERSONAL IDENTITY AS MISSIONARIES AND STEWARDS

You are not your own;
you were bought with a price.

I Corinthians 6.19

We are ambassadors for Christ,
since God is making his appeal through us.

II Corinthians 5.20

As we take on Jesus' character and holiness and begin to see ourselves as sons and daughters of God, as members of his body, the Church, and as temples of the Holy Spirit, we also take on God's passion for drawing others into a life with himself. Our priorities change! That, or God has more work to do. In fact, we should begin to love one another freely and with joy, even at significant personal cost. And we embrace a missionary life of interceding for, and helping, others to know God.

Our lives are not our own: we are to be about the business of Heaven! A mature disciple also recognizes that everything comes from God – all that one has and all that one is. God's power makes us see our very consciousness and human freedom as well as material possessions, education, upbringing (such as it may be), current position, resources, time, health, energy - simply everything - as gifts to further God's plans for our lives and those around us. In short, a mature disciple approaches his life as a steward of God's gifts. What does God expect of us, based on the parable of the talents in Matthew 25.14-30?

_____

_____

_____

Depending on our circumstances, many of us will have time and resources beyond what is required to care for our families to help others: both through works of mercy, serving the Church, and evangelism (see the chapters on Mission below). Whatever our circumstances, as God transforms us into the likeness of his Son, caring for those around us and helping people come into a relationship with God becomes our overarching concerns.

Take another look at Luke 15, the chapter about what causes Heaven to rejoice. Indeed, the business (and the joy) of Heaven is bringing people into Heaven! As God's sons or daughters, we take up this Family Business: we take on the identity of missionaries! Throughout his pontificate in too many places to cite, John Paul II strenuously exhorted every Catholic to take up the missionary mandate of Jesus! The U.S. Conference of Catholic Bishops also stresses our identity and duty as missionaries in pastoral documents like *Go and Make Disciples*.

WORLDVIEW

*If then you have been raised with Christ, **seek the things that are above**, where Christ is, seated at the right hand of God. Set your minds on things that are above, not on things that are on earth. For you have died, and your life is hid with Christ in God. When Christ who is our life appears, then you also will appear with him in glory.* Colossians 3.2-4

Creation itself will be set free from its bondage to decay and obtain the glorious liberty of the children of God. Romans 8.21

Now let's consider the "world" or popular culture. Every worldview is based on a set of values, explicitly or implicitly. Worldly values are expressed in movies, TV, casual conversations, magazines, and internet sites among other places, and include the common ideas on being happy, getting ahead, sex, money, power, relationships, self fulfillment, etc. List and briefly describe some important values of the world:

1. _____
   _____

2. _____
   _____

3. _____
   _____

Although there is some overlap, God's values generally differ from the world's. He primarily sees the potential for tremendous beauty and goodness in every human being and longs for a deep union with each of us. Perhaps God's main work is drawing us into, and making us suitable for, an eternal relationship with him. The *world* is a place for human beings to learn about and exercise their free will in choosing what is good, true and beautiful. Of course, it's also chock full of generally boring but sometimes spectacularly bad choices. Ill-use of ourselves and others (sin) grieves God. Beyond the beauty of creation, God sees little more in the *world* than persons either embracing or rejecting his plan for them to be with him, to become like him and to love what he loves[a]. God sees that those who reject his plan ultimately change into creatures unfit for his company and that of his people. God also sees that some angels who have rejected his plans strive against his plans for us but that the angels with Him (and saints in Heaven) join the battle on our behalf. Chapters 1-3 of Part I and Chapter 3 of Part II discussed some of these realities.

God put us on earth to know him and to transform us into a creature resembling himself. Our time on earth is a time for growth and transformation. Aside from this eternal perspective, little makes sense. We will die and then God will judge us on whether we have accepted his forgiveness and the grace to become the men and women he wishes us to be – in relationship with Him, coming to resemble His goodness, and loving others as He himself does. This grace necessarily issues fruit (Matthew 25); faith without works is a dead faith.

American Catholics no longer – if we ever did – live in a society that reinforces and supports God's plan for our lives. The voracious competition for our values, time and resources, and how we think about almost every aspect of life is nothing less than a spiritual battle for our very souls. Society in turn feeds and challenges us with materialistic and individualistic values and worldview. How we actually spend our time and discretionary resources usually indicates whether we are living more under the influence of the *world* or according to God's plan for our lives.

---

[a] Persons lacking an explicit relationship with God in Christ may implicitly although imperfectly embrace God's plan by following their consciences, loving and caring for others, working and building goods things – all of which please God.

DISCUSSION QUESTIONS

1. How would you like people to remember you when you die?

_____

_____

_____

_____

_____

_____

2. What do you find most troubling about what the world tells us to be? Why?

_____

_____

_____

_____

_____

_____

3. What do you think John Paul II means by a "civilization of love"? How can you contribute?

_____

_____

_____

_____

_____

_____

7 - Life Choices & Daily Routine

Then Jesus told his disciples, *If any man would come after me, let him deny himself and take up his cross and follow me. For whoever would save his life will lose it, and whoever loses his life for my sake will find it.*
For what will it profit a man, if he gains the whole world and forfeits his life?
Or what shall a man give in return for his life?

Matthew 16.24-26

What does selling everything, laying down our lives and following Jesus actually mean in our daily lives? If following Jesus means following his plan, we must ask our self whether every aspect of our life corresponds to his plan. In the real world, we talk about theory moving into practice as being "where the rubber meets the road". This chapter considers where being a Catholic disciple meets the real world of our choices, time, relationships and resources – which together make up our "pattern of life".

All the decisions related to how we spend our time and resources largely determine our particular **Pattern of Life** or way of life. Our Pattern of Life is comprised of four major components:

- Life Choices
- Daily Routine
- Relationships with Family, Friends, and Others
- Resources

This chapter considers the first two elements of our pattern of life while Chapter 8 considers relationships and resources.

A QUESTION OF CONSISTENCY

The overarching question for a disciple is how much our Pattern of Life *supports or expresses* God's plan for our life. What are the **Core Elements of God's plan for our life**? They include:

- A strong prayer and sacramental life
- A Christian personal identity and worldview
- A life of holiness and Christian character
- A life of love and caring for others
- A strong marriage and family life
- Explicitly Christian fraternal relationships

- A life of mission through intercessory prayer and an eagerness to share about Jesus to others

The scope of this section is limited to asking how our Pattern of Life supports or expresses the core elements of God's plan for our life. How to take on and live out these core elements is one of the goals of the companion to this book, *Made to Be Like Him*.

LIFE CHOICES

Let each of you lead the life that the Lord has assigned you, to which God has called you.

I Corinthians 8.17

Life Choices are major directional decisions such as to one's vocation and career, the location of one's post-secondary schooling, where one lives, choice of a spouse, the type of house in which one lives, how many children to rear, savings and retirement plans, etc. Depending on how old you are, many of these choices may already be made and only some may be changed easily. However, unless we are in the final years of our life, we probably have at least a few major life decisions left relating to work, savings rate and retirement.

What major life choices do you face over the next twenty years?

1. _____

2. _____

3. _____

4. _____

For one of these life choices, describe how your choice may effect the core elements of God's plan for your life (see previous page for listing)?

_____
_____
_____
_____

DAILY ROUTINE

Whatever you eat or drink, or whatever you do, do everything for the glory of God.

I Corinthians 10.31

Our **Daily Routine** is determined to some degree by our Life Choices and involves work, prayer, leisure, relationships, serving others, etc., but also depends on the priorities we set and our self-discipline. Of course, the demands of school, work, family and outside commitments can surge from time to time and upset the best laid plans of mice and men! However, our life choices and day to day priorities generally determine our daily routines. For example, how hard we work and how much we play largely determines how much time we have for prayer, caring for our family and others, and maintaining life-giving relationships with other Christians.

The key question is how our daily routine supports and expresses the core elements of God's plan for our lives – and whether we need to change or tweak our routines. Consider how well your daily and weekly activities align with God's plan for you (these questions are meant as primers that hopefully spawn additional questions more applicable to your life).

- ✓ Do we draw out, or linger too much over, our waking up routine?

- ✓ How much do we read the paper each day or surf the web for sports, news, or other interests?

- ✓ How much time do we devote to email?

- ✓ How do we putter away our time?

- ✓ What do we read; what shows or movies do we watch?

- ✓ How often and how long do we stay late at work? ... why?

- ✓ How many sports and activities are we (and our kids) involved in?

- ✓ How are we spending Sundays?

- ✓ Do we realistically have time for serving people outside our immediate family?

- ✓ Should we consider spending less time watching or playing sports, of curtailing some other leisure activity, or even downsizing our work or our financial life?

- ✓ How much time do we devote each day to prayer and Scripture reading?

Take an "inventory" of the routine activities that make up your days and weeks and consider how each activity supports or detracts from the core elements of God's plan for your life. Then, put a "+" under any core elements that the activity expresses or reinforces, a "-" under any core elements that the activity undermines.

Dailey Activities	Prayer & Sacramental Life	Christian Identity & Worldview	Holiness and Christian Character	Caring for Others	Strong Family Life	Christian Fellowship	Life of Mission
Doing the laundry			+	+			

Weekly Activities

	Prayer & Sacramental Life	Christian Identity & Worldview	Holiness and Christian Character	Caring for Others	Strong Family Life	Christian Fellowship	Life of Mission
Watching sex-laden TV shows		–	–				

Now consider some additional activities that could express or strengthen the core elements of God's plan for your life:

Core Element	Potential Activity

Strong Prayer & Sacramental Life
- _____
- _____

Christian Identity & Worldview
- _____
- _____

Holiness & Christian Character
- _____
- _____

Caring for others
- _____
- _____

Strong family life
- _____
- _____

Christian Fellowship
- _____
- _____

Life of Mission
- _____
- _____

WHAT'S YOUR EXPERIENCE?

1. Consider a couple of activities that conflict with or undermine a core element of God's plan for your life. Describe how these activities oppose the given core element.

_____

_____

_____

_____

_____

_____

_____

2. Consider a couple of activities that express or strengthen a core element of God's plan for your life. Describe how these activities align with the given core element.

_____

_____

_____

_____

_____

_____

_____

8 - Relationships & Resources

Maintain a constant love for one another . . . serve one another with whatever gift each of your has received.   I Peter 4.8-9

As discussed in the last chapter, our particular **Pattern of Life** or way of life is made up of four general areas. The key question for a disciple is how well our Pattern of Life supports God's plan for our life. The reverse is also true: as we embrace God's plan for our life, our Pattern of Life will also change: growing in our identity as sons and daughters of God will doubtless influence how we relate to others. As we come to understand that the most crucial thing about life is having a relationship with God, our use of time will begin to reflect this central priority. And of course, embracing one aspect of God's plan for our life reinforces other aspects. For example, as we take on a daily prayer life – experiencing the Father's love and grace regularly – we should grow in holiness and our identity as his sons and daughters.

Pattern of Life   ### God's Plan for Our Life

- Life Choices
- Daily Routine
- Personal Relationships
- Resources

- A strong prayer and sacramental Life
- A Christian self-understanding (or identity) and worldview
- A life of holiness and Christian character
- A life of love and service towards others, starting with one's family
- A strong marriage and family life
- Explicitly Christian fraternal relationships
- A life of mission through intercessory prayer and sharing Jesus with others

The last chapter briefly considered how Life Choices and Daily Routine relate to God's plan for our life; this chapter begins by briefly considering the role of our Personal Relationships. Most people control at least some of the activities that make up our Daily Routine. All of us control with whom we spend leisure time outside the family. This chapter concludes by introducing the question of resources and personal finances[a].

BEYOND RECREATIONAL FRIENDSHIP

From now on, therefore, we regard no one from a human point of view; even though we once regarded Christ from a human point of view, we regard him thus no longer. Therefore, if any one is in Christ, he is a new creation; the old has passed away, behold, the new has come.

II Corinthians 5.16-17

Consider for a moment the big picture: How do we relate to your family and friends? Do we have friends that encourage your relationship with God? Do you have friends that undermine our life with God? Are we helping others regularly? To whom can we turn for help when in need? Do we experience the joy of friendship? Is our family life all that God intends it? Dare we compare our family life to that of

---

He's not Goofy, He's my Brother

I thought the guy was a jerk. Well, not a jerk, but at least nerdy. He was tall and lanky. I didn't like his humor. Meet my brother (in Christ) Dave and my new roommate in the fall of 1982. We already got on each other's nerves in the small group we shared, and now we roomed together in a dorm for the sake of evangelism!

To my surprise, by the end of that year we became best friends, closer than blood brothers in a certain way - though still quite different! While Dave moved away, I still consider him a best friend and deeply esteem him. I can't tell you how many men I have grown close to as brothers in Christ since then. I feel like a man grown wealthy with such brotherly friendships.

---

the Trinity, as the *Catechism* invites[b]? Or liken love for our spouse to Christ's love, out of which he lays down his life for the Church[c]? This section considers friendships while Chapter 10 examines families.

Most of us love to hang out or do stuff with certain people, but many of these relationships have little depth and might be called *Recreational Friendships*. Recreational friendships tend to start and stop while talking over coffee, going to the bar, watching sports, or perhaps at a book club. Recreational friendships usually end when the going gets tough, when you need some help, or simply when the common interest dies. Nothing wrong with recreational friendships, just don't build your life around them or expect them to yield long-term joy. God wants to give us both great joy and encouragement in living for him from deep brotherly and sisterly relationships.

---

[a] Again, a more extensive treatment of these topics may be found in, *Made to be Like Him*; check www.GodsPlanforYourLife.org for availability of this study.
[b] CCC 2205.
[c] Ephesians 5.25.

BROTHERS & SISTERS IN CHRIST

As for the saints in the land, they are the noble, in whom is all my delight.

Psalm 16.3

If we're drawing near to God, we should notice the other people heading in the same direction: they're our brothers and sisters through our common Baptism in Christ. If Baptism makes us sons and daughters of God – we pick up many siblings in the process! On one hand, they are (or will eventually be) a source of great joy. Next to life with himself, God's greatest gifts are relationships with others who are near him. As God makes us like himself we, in turn, are sources of joy to each other. I know it sounds a little too good to be true, but we have a Big God with a Big Plan backed by Big Power and Big Commitment on his part.

On the other hand, we love one another, from washing each other's feet to laying down our lives (and everything in between), in direct obedience to the Lord's oft repeated teaching[a]. We help each other with the practical challenges of everyday life, console each other, show kindness - in a word, love our neighbor as ourselves.

I guess on what would be a third hand, God uses us to encourage and help one another live as Christians and to embrace God's entire plan for our life. Many Christians have found joining with others in small groups focused on discipleship – that is, embracing God's plan for our life – to be extremely fruitful. I, for one, doubt I would have continued to embrace God's plan for my life without the encouragement I found in my first couple of small groups.

LOVING OTHERS

If you love those who love you, if you do good to those who do good to you, if you lend to those from whom you hope to receive, what credit is that to you? ... Love your enemies, do good, lend, expecting nothing in return. Be merciful as your heavenly father in merciful.

Luke 6.32-36

Aside from our brothers and sisters in Christ and perhaps even more so, God calls us to love those who don't yet know him. While we look and pray for opportunities to help people discover the greatest treasure and joy in life – a relationship with God – we mostly just care for material or emotional needs. Simply esteeming and valuing people from our heart is a profound way of loving others, although caring for our "neighbor" will often be inconvenient and even costly. Of

---

[a] See, for example, John 13-15.

course, as we see in Matthew 25, God expects us to love the particularly needy as if they were Christ himself.

A QUESTION OF ALIGNMENT

While we love and care first for our spouses and families, to the extent we have time and resources left over, we care for others in tangible ways. More on this in the next chapter.

Consider how well our friendships and acquaintances align with God's plan for us (these questions are really meant as primers that hopefully spawn additional questions more applicable to your life).

- ✓ What specific things sustain and strengthen our marriages such as date nights and regular discussions of family life?

- ✓ What relationships specifically support God's plan for your life?

- ✓ Are you relaxed enough to express kindness in the chance encounters of daily life, even to a retail clerk whose "on-the-job training" is making you late?

- ✓ Are you regularly interceding for God's plan to take root in those around you?

Let's take another "inventory", this time of our friends and acquaintances, and consider how these relationships tend to support or detract from the core aspects of God's plan for us.

Friends	Prayer & Sacramental Life	Christian Identity & Worldview	Holiness and Christian Character	Caring for Others	Strong Family Life	Christian Fellowship	Life of Mission
Cousin Rick			+		+	+	

Acquaintances	Prayer & Sacramental Life	Christian Identity & Worldview	Holiness and Christian Character	Caring for Others	Strong Family Life	Christian Fellowship	Life of Mission
Co-worker		−	−				

RESOURCES . . . MONEY, MONEY, MONEY

The fourth measure of our Pattern of Life is resources, the most tangible of which is *mullah*. Money is more easily measured than the other three elements of our Pattern of Life: Life Choices, Daily Routine, and Personal Relationships. Like the other elements, choices related to money are deeply intertwined with our personal identity, what we value in life, our goals for life, how deliberately we approach life, and, in general, how we embrace God's plan for our lives. In regard to money and resources, this chapter is limited to posing a few general questions.

> **Which Master?**
>
> No one can serve two masters; for either he will hate the one and love the other, or he will be devoted to the one and despise the other. You cannot serve God and money.   Matthew 6.24

How does your use of money reflect and support God's plan for your life? Name three specific instances:

1. _____

2. _____

3. _____

How does your use of money undermine God's plan for your life? Name three specific instances:

1. _____

2. _____

3. _____

SUMMING IT ALL UP

As we have seen in this section, God wants to transform nearly every aspect our lives in very concrete ways. Rather than a figure of speech, God literally wants to make us new creations after the pattern of his own son, Jesus. For you diagram buffs, the following is one way to picture the various aspects of transformation.

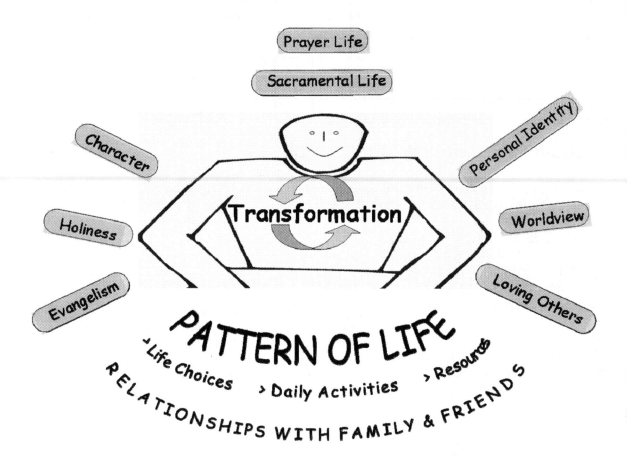

WHAT'S YOUR EXPERIENCE?

1. Consider a relationship that *conflicts with or undermines* a core element of God's plan for your life.   Describe how the relationship opposes the given core element.

   _____

   _____

   _____

   _____

2. Consider a relationship that *expresses or strengthens* a core element of God's plan for your life.   Describe how the relationship aligns with the given core element.

   _____

   _____

   _____

   _____

LOVING WHOM GOD LOVES (MISSION)

"As the Father has sent me, so I send you"

9 – The Joy of Loving Others

The Mother Theresa Syndrome

Being a liberal arts major, I soon realized what a duck-out-of-water I was in business school. Desiring a family and without the prospect of gainful employment, I found myself in a school I hated – yet I stayed. Though already a practicing Catholic, I was hardly immune to the allure of fame, fortune and power in the world of business. But where was the joy in my classmates? Some found joy in creative course work. God certainly gives pleasure in exercising his gifts – which is true in any kind of work we do however aesthetic and creative (most business schoolwork involves little of either). While my classmates had lots of drive and passion, I saw little joy. Against this backdrop, I experienced something of an epiphany while traveling to Asia after graduation.

I spent a good deal of the eighteen-hour plane ride to Singapore reading about a figure soaring in popularity at the time: Mother Theresa. The contrast between Mother Theresa and her gang of nuns and my business school buddies couldn't have been greater. A larger culture clash is hard to imagine. Talk about hero worship - go hang out in a top business school for a few days, where everybody wants to be a *gazillionaire*. Everybody wants to run a major corporation. One spends much of the two years picturing yourself in different roles of power, imagining people looking up to you and thinking about what wonderful and creative things you'll soon be doing . . . how much you'll be loved (or envied) for your accomplishments and position - all this to speak nothing of the gratifications of making and spending tons of money. There was little confusion in business school about what makes you happy: a job with fat pay and a promising career track. Did I mention making money, lots of money.

Now cut to me alone for an eighteen-hour flight, quite isolated from the business school culture. Reading story after story about this diminutive lady spending four hours a day on her knees in prayer, ten hours caring for the worst of the worst, then refreshing herself in the squalor of her dingy quarters over a bowl of watery soup . . . followed by more prayer and a short night on straw. A pretty riveting and ecstatic existence, wouldn't you say?

I didn't think so. Certainly not the American recipe for joy and happiness. Yet a certain joy sparkles – even flashes– from her face, filling the room. Young women, from good homes and bad, swell her ranks of do-gooders. Many see in her the face of joy and the face of Christ. Many great people of the world sought her out; some came to faith in Christ through her witness. I had rarely met such joy as Mother Theresa's and the Sisters of Charity. If anyone was happy on earth, paradoxically, it was these women! A more perfect opposite of the typical business school grad is hard to find (not that we are really such a bad lot).

LIKE FATHER, LIKE SON: JOY IN LOVING OTHERS

I delight to do your will, O my God; your law is within my heart.

Psalm 40.8

How do you account for the culture-defying joy of Mother Theresa? It's the old answer – it's in the genes. Mother Theresa's genes, however, aren't unique; in fact, I'm actually talking about some pretty amazing genes common to us all. Read Genesis 1.26-27 and describe what it says about our "genetic" makeup:

_____

_____

_____

_____

You didn't really need to read this excerpt from the Creation story to get the point. We already know from our study in the last chapter that God makes us a new creation after the pattern of Jesus. Does God making us like Jesus change our motivations and life goals? As we more and more reflect the image of Christ, do we also begin doing what Jesus does? One can only chuckle at the force of this logic.

→ **Why ?????**

→ **How ?????**

→ **Won't it be boring ?????**

On a certain level, the proper response to God's plan for us to not only *become like Jesus* but to *do what Jesus does* is sheer terror. In fact, God wishes so thoroughly to transform our hearts that we come *to love* who he loves.

> *God's love has been poured into our hearts through the Holy Spirit which has been given to us.*
>
> Romans 5.5

WHY? – YOU CAN'T HELP IT!

Since God made us in his image – lost in the Garden of Eden through sin but restored by being born anew in Christ – as we conform more and more to this image, we can't help but loving who God loves. God has designed or programmed for loving others as He does. What are God's basic motivations and goals? How do John 3.16-17 and I John 4.7-12 describe these?

_____

_____

_____

_____

Of course, on our bad days we can sometimes, shall we say, *override the program*. Until God transforms away our "bad days": even if we don't "feel like it" we love others in obedience to Jesus command. What does Jesus command in John 15.12-13?

121

How? – By God's Power

The *Catechism* puts it this way, picking up one of the main themes of John 15:

> The Savior himself comes to love, in us, his Father and his brethren, our Father and our brethren. His person becomes, through the Spirit, the living and interior rule of our activity.
>
> (CCC 2074)

Indeed, loving others is a God-thing – meaning that God not only has to point the way but also supply the power. Read John 15 verses 1-5 and 12-13. Yes, there it is again. Repetition may madden, but I bet you've got this passage down by now. I say you can't get enough of a good thing. What is the key to loving others according to these passages? How do we accomplish this?

_____

_____

_____

You may wish to review Chapter 3 on Tapping God's Power and Chapter 4 on Fighting the Good Fight.

Boring . . . or Source of Great Joy?

God delights in the human beings he has created – see Genesis 1.26-7. God also delights in bringing people to himself – take a look at the great joy of the father welcoming home his once evil son in the story of the Prodigal Son (Luke 15).

What's Dr. Seuss got to do with it?
Sam cajoles his reluctant buddy into trying green eggs and ham: "Try them! Try them! And you may. Try them and you may, I say".
Just give loving others a try.
Your response may parallel that of Sam's buddy: "I do so like green eggs and ham! Thank you! Thank you, Sam-I-am."

Wonder what motivates God? Isn't "love" *something you do*? Actually, I think it's ultimately more like *something you are* (or become). Now, why would anyone wish to become like Mother Theresa? I think the simple reason is that it ultimately gives us joy. Of course, if the person we love doesn't require

_____

_____

_____

_____

_____

the supreme sacrifice like Jesus' death on the Cross– so much the better. If we really love someone, we cherish their good above our own and it gives us joy.

Look at the strange paternal love that drives parents to make sacrifices for the sake of bettering their children or to rescue their baby from a burning house. Ultimately, we can't know *why* loving us gives God pleasure or why loving others so fills the Sisters of Charity with joy. All we can say is – *it does!*   It's just how God is, and consequently, how we ourselves are programmed. Being made in the image of God, "the practice of goodness is accompanied by spontaneous spiritual joy and moral beauty"[a]. This joy or pleasure comes from the work of Christ in us through the Holy Spirit:

> Moral perfection consists in man's being moved to the good not by his will alone, but also by his sensitive appetite, as in the words of the psalm: "My heart and flesh sing for joy to the living God." We live a law of love that makes us act out of the love infused by the Holy Spirit. (CCC 1770, 1971)

The "spontaneity" with which spiritual joy and moral beauty will accompany our practice of goodness will vary with each individual based on factors such as personality, legacy sin, etc.   In other words, it may take a bit of time before we rejoice over doing the dishes or changing diapers!

WHAT'S YOUR EXPERIENCE?

1. Describe an experience of joy, satisfaction or pleasure in helping other people.

    _____
    _____
    _____
    _____

2. Would you expect to have more joy over scrimping and saving in order to help feed a hungry person or to buy an expensive car for your child? Why?

    _____
    _____
    _____

---

[a] CCC 2500.

10 – Our Mission: Caring for Others & Evangelism

Love your neighbor as yourself   Luke 10.27

You too go into the vineyard   Matthew 20.7

As God transforms our lives to resemble that of Jesus' in terms of who we are, how we think, what we feel, and how we relate to the Father and other human beings, we also come to love whom God loves. The godly sense of loving something is to ascribe to it infinite value and relate to it accordingly. Loving gold implies hoarding gold. Loving others implies caring for others and advancing their interests. Let's consider some of the ways God would have us do this. Jesus' love has two practical dimensions: caring for their needs and bringing people into a relationship with God.

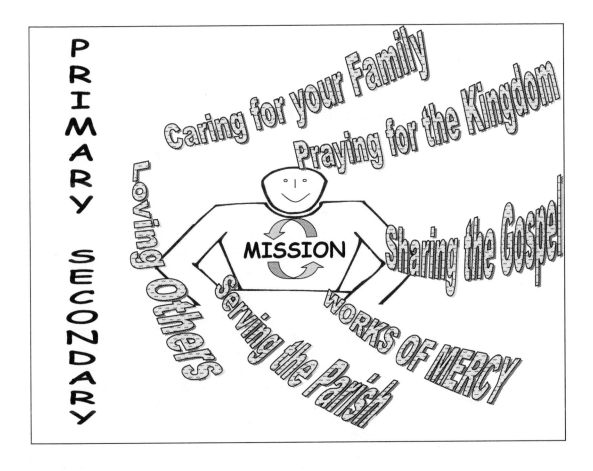

1. FAMILIES FIRST

Therefore a man leaves his father and his mother and cleaves to his wife,
and they become one flesh. Genesis 2.24

God first calls us to love those who are in our immediate midst as he loves them. We are to *love our spouses* as Christ loves the Church. We are to *love one another* as Jesus loves us, again, from washing one another's feet to laying down our lives. We are to *care for our children* just as God would. Therefore, we first express our love for those who are already in our midst, foremost those whom God has already entrusted to us, our immediate families.

What are some practical ways you have loved and cared for your parents, spouse or children in the last week?

❖ _____

❖ _____

❖ _____

2. INTERCESSION: THY KINGDOM COME

Read Matthew 6.8-15. Ponder the meaning of the first petition Jesus asks us to pray (verse 10). What do you suppose this means?

_____
_____
_____
_____
_____

Praying for God's kingdom to come probably points to several things but there can be little doubt the primary meaning is *for others to enter the kingdom of God* – "may *your kingdom come*" (into the lives of every human being). Far from being the exclusive role of monks, God calls us all to enter a nonstop life of praying for other people to embrace God's plan for their lives. Interceding for others is the stuff of daily commutes, trips to the grocery store, even while showering. A life of intercession supplements rather than replaces a more concentrated daily time of prayer. While we might begin the day with Mass, Scripture reading or a personal prayer time, we fill odd bits of time throughout the day with intercession. Such a life of daily intercession is no less important to bringing others into the riches of life with God than the preaching of a great evangelist. A life of daily intercession should characterize the homebound person no less or more than the career evangelist or your parish priest. Intercession is a tangible and crucial way all of the people of God are called to join in the saving priestly work of Jesus.

Review your intercessory list from Part I, Chapter 5.

3. SHARING JESUS WITH OTHERS

The most valuable gift that the Church can offer to the bewildered and restless world of our time is to form within it Christians who are confirmed in what is essential and who are humbly joyful in their faith.[a]

We are like the person who found the treasure and sold everything to possess it (Matthew 13.44). The treasure is our relationship with God and his people, a treasure so rich and overflowing that giving it away can't diminish it. God wants our hearts to burn for others to possess the surpassing riches of knowing God. All disciples of Jesus should be ready to share their faith[b]. Read Matthew 28.18 to see what Jesus says more specifically – What exactly does Jesus command? How can you respond to this command?

_____

_____

_____

_____

_____

_____

As we can see, Jesus concludes his earthly ministry by sending his disciples forth to bring all nations into a relationship with him. The overall theme of John Paul II's pontificate may be *New Evangelism*, the call to bring people into a relationship with God through Jesus.

Well, easier said than done, as the adage goes . . . except that Jesus never asked anyone to share his good news without some help. Read Acts 1.4-8. What kind of big-time help does Jesus offer?

_____

_____

This help is available to us as well[c]. How to tap into it? Just like in becoming like Jesus, in order to share about Jesus we have to ask for God's power. We ask for love and confidence in our

---

[a] *On Catechesis in our Time*, paragraph 61.
[b] I Peter 3.15, CCC 900, 905.
[c] See CCC 767-768. Some Catholics experience an even more profound outpouring of God's Holy Spirit – see the Charismatic Renewal; even these gifts are available to those who earnestly ask Jesus for them.

sharing. Above all, we ask God to draw specific people to himself and then look for opportunities to share gently our "good news" about Jesus (the Gospel) with them.

List five people to begin praying for right now (and continue to do so at least weekly):

- ❖ _____
- ❖ _____
- ❖ _____
- ❖ _____
- ❖ _____

How about the basics of sharing the gospel with others? You don't have to be perfect nor have everything all figured out. The only requirement is embracing and treasuring your life with God. The main point is God calls all of us to be ready to share, not just a priest or professional evangelist. In fact, better to avoid fancy theological language, whoever you are. Best simply to share about how you came into, or became more deeply aware of, your relationship with God and to share some way in which God has changed you. Of course, *some* prep is helpful. My hope is that this booklet, especially Part I, Chapters 1-3 and Part II, Chapter 2 helps you learn how to share the Gospel with others.[a]

4. SERVING OUTSIDE THE HOME

Share in suffering for the gospel　　　　　　　　II Timothy 1.8

God expects us to align soberly our Pattern of Life with his priorities, as discussed in Chapters 7 and 8. After aligning our lives with God's plan many will find time for serving God's kingdom outside of our homes, at least during some periods of our lives. First, we love whoever happens to cross our paths (Luke 10.30-37). While we have to be wise about not giving away time and money we don't have, the Lord wants us to care for the neighbor in need who chances across our path. Many of us will be able to get involved outside our homes in ways beyond the chance need or crisis of a "neighbor".

Read Matthew 25:31-46 and list the specific ways that God will judge what we do with the incredible resources he lavishes upon our society[b]:

---

[a] Some practical tools are available on www.GodsPlanforYourLife.org. You should also check with your pastor for any training that is available at your parish.

[b] What! This author is nuts! Yeah, I know you are probably busy and stressed out over lack of time with your loved ones and stretching to make the next mortgage payment. That's why I saved this nugget till the end of the study. Nonetheless, objectively, Americans consume something like five to ten times more than the average person on the planet (excluding those who are starving). Each of us are going to have to answer for what we do with the resources that are obviously way more than is necessary for basic life. Let Matthew 7.13-14 and Matthew 25 be your guides,

- ❖ _____
- ❖ _____
- ❖ _____
- ❖ _____

The opportunities for those able to serve outside their homes on a regular basis may be grouped into the following categories. List some specific ways to serve for each category, e.g., becoming involved in the Knights of Columbus as a Work of Mercy (raises money for charity):

- Evangelism (perhaps the most pressing area)

    1) _____

    2) _____

    3) _____

- Supporting the internal life of the parish and the Church

    1) _____

    2) _____

    3) _____

- Works of Mercy, whether sponsored by your parish or otherwise

    1) _____

    2) _____

    3) _____

APPLICATION QUESTIONS

1. Take some time to consider soberly and prayerfully your ability to serve outside your home. What daily, weekly or monthly activities, if any, might you replace with time spent serving others outside the home?

---

together with the countless Saints the Church holds up as examples. We can't outdo God in generosity: see Matthew 19.16-30.

_____

_____

2. Which category and specific services most interest you? Do you feel God calling you to something particular? Why?

_____

_____

_____

_____

11 - Celebration & the Road Ahead

I hope that God has worked powerfully in your lives. "Basic construction" of your life as a disciple should be well underway, if not complete, including the following elements:

- A strong prayer and sacramental life
- A Christian personal identity and worldview
- A life of holiness and Christian character
- A life of love and caring for others
- A strong marriage and family life
- Explicitly Christian fraternal relationships
- A life of mission through intercessory prayer and an eagerness to share about Jesus to others

Our foundation is conversion while a solid prayer and sacramental life fuels our ongoing transformation and life of charity and mission. For our part, we have put the Lord on the throne of our lives, yielding ourselves without reservation. We have aligned our Pattern of Life with God's plan in terms of our life choices, daily routine, relationships with others and personal finances.

This chapter has just two exercises, the first one being a celebration.

A CELEBRATIVE TOAST

Now that you see with spiritual eyes you probably realize that God has all sorts of plans for further "improvements and additions" to your life. Perfecting the life of holiness, prayer, serving others, getting our life in perfect order, etc., will take a bit longer than the months that you've invested in this book. Perhaps you have had to confront some very deep hurts or personal weaknesses due to earlier patterns of sin that will need some significant help.

Your life of discipleship is probably going very well thus far – rejoice and be glad. Some of you, however, may be somewhat frustrated by the slowness of progress or from legacy sin (see the end of Chapter 6), be of good cheer. You have made substantial progress and you have a heavenly Father who has counted every hair of your head – you are extremely precious to him, whatever your shortcomings or problems. God is deeply committed to fully transforming our life, however difficult and long that may take, with great love and gentleness.

Not So Humble Thanksgiving!

Oh God, thank you for making me so perfect. so loving, so kind, a model for my men's group, a light to those in darkness . . .

If you have been working through this book with some other disciples, make this meeting celebrative. You may wish to have a nice dinner together or simply bring some particularly festive drinks and desserts. Let your time of prayer together be primarily thanksgiving for all that God has done for you. Honor what God has done in each of your lives.

Take some time to consider three areas of your life that God has transformed.

➤ _____

➤ _____

➤ _____

Consider how God has worked in each member of your group. List growth in a particular virtue, holiness, changes in how they live, how they have been encouraging, etc.

Group Member	Area of Growth or Transformation
_____	_____
_____	_____
_____	_____
_____	_____
_____	_____
_____	_____

I suggest thanking God for the ways he has worked in your life during your group's time of thanksgiving prayer. Of course, do so in a spirit of humility! Then, during your meal or dessert and drinks, honor each other for ways in which God has been at work. Make such honoring of each other a tradition on your birthdays a tradition.

THE ROAD AHEAD

So where do we go from here? Do you wish to continue meeting as a group? Take some time to review the "Discipleship Map" on the next page. While your group may wish to take a short break from "discipleship stuff", consider what area you would be most interested in working on next.

List a few discipleship topics you are interested in pursuing further:

➢ _____

➢ _____

➢ _____

A more comprehensive treatment of discipleship is also contained in the following studies[a]:

- *Made for Worship* - Considers the Mass thru the schema of "Being with God, Becoming like Him and Loving Whom He Loves", particularly looking at the scriptural roots and emphasizing personally entering into worship and personally embracing God's transforming power of the Mass. Like *Made for Joy*, *Made for Worship* intends, in part, to foster personal conversion.
- *Made to be Like Him* – builds upon the transformation chapters contained in *Made for Joy*. Topics include Christian personal identity and worldview, character, virtues, fruit of the Spirit, emotions, the Beatitudes and adopting a Christian Pattern of Life.
- *Made for Fellowship* - a brief reflection on Christian friendship as well as practical approaches to living close, fraternal Christian relationships.
- *Made for Love* - builds upon the mission chapters of *Made for Joy* and includes helps in determining your area of gifting and service as well as training modules for evangelism.

---

[a] These titles are part of the "Embracing God's Plan for Your Life" series. See www.GodsPlanforYourLife.org for more information on these titles, some of which are forthcoming.

Discipleship Map
A Listing of Transformation and Mission Topics

Aspects of Transformation

- Develop a strong prayer and sacramental life
    - Develop a life of prayer and Scripture study
    - Understand the Mass and other sacraments
- Form a Christian Personal Identity and Worldview
    - Core Aspects of a Believer's Identity
    - Elements of a Christian Worldview
- Grow in Holiness and the Character of Christ
    - Basics: Sin, Conscience, Grace and Holiness
    - Character Transformation: freedom from serious sin; practice of Christian virtues; and growth in the fruit of the spirit and emotional maturity
- Develop a Christian Pattern of Life
    - Elements: Life Choices, Daily Routine, Relationships and Resources
    - Align one's Pattern of Life to support the Core Elements
        - A strong prayer and sacramental life
        - A Christian personal identity and worldview
        - A life of holiness and Christian character
        - A life of love and caring for others
        - A strong marriage and family life
        - Explicitly Christian fraternal relationships
        - A life of mission
- Live as Stewards of God's Gifts
- Develop strong Fraternal Christian Friendships
- Develop a strong Marriage and Family Life

Mission

- Love your "neighbors" by cheerfully helping them
- Receive general training on Intercession and Evangelism
- Identify and embrace a mission (for those able to serve beyond caring for their family): evangelism; supporting internal parish life; or works of mercy

Suggestions for Group Study

1. Agree on a discussion group leader (facilitator). The facilitator helps people who talk too little talk more and those who talk a lot, well, talk less! The facilitator also helps maintain the group's focus on the given chapter, avoid bogging down on peripheral issues, and maintain a positive atmosphere. In fact, these are the responsibilities common to whole group.

   The facilitator is not (normally) a theological or biblical expert. But the facilitator will plan ahead on how to pace the group to ponder and discuss the interpretation and application questions in each chapter. The facilitator may download facilitator guides for each chapter from www.GodsPlanforYourLife.org   or   www.ParishLifeServices.org.

2. Open with Prayer. The prayer may be the *Lord's Prayer*, one or more worshipful songs, or any other type of prayer. The emphasis should be on inviting God to enliven the discussion with the Holy Spirit – after all, the whole point is to encounter the living God and allow Him to transform and inspire you!

3. Spend at least ½ hour preparing each chapter. Of course, sometimes life does get hectic and we don't prepare as much as we hope. Normally, there is time to further ponder the interpretation and discussion questions when the group meets. As well, selections of each chapter may be read during the meeting.

4. Discuss the material in a positive way. Smile and be attentive to each other. Encourage each other to know the Lord more deeply and embrace His plan for our life! Be sure to provide time for each person to speak.

5. Keep the Focus on Jesus and the Holy Spirit. The focus is on practically applying God's word in your life, not deep theological enquiry. Focus on how to appropriate God's grace in your life rather than subtle theological questions. When challenging questions come up, appoint someone from the group to ask your pastor, the overall leader, or simply consult the Catechism of the Catholic Church.

6. Maintain Candor and Confidentiality. Discussing your relationship with God involves our personal life and feelings, as does discussing how to more fully embrace God's plan for our lives. Often, men find it easier to share with other men and likewise with women – consider splitting up by sex.

7. Pray for one another. Close each meeting by each person making a prayer request for themselves or others, then the others praying silently for fifteen seconds. Close with either the *Lord's Prayer* or a *Hail Mary*. Pray for each others' requests at least one time during the week.

8. Start and finish promptly. People may linger afterwards or all agree to continue the discussion, but people should always be free to leave at the agreed upon time.

For Further Study

GENERAL

This book generally quotes from the Revised Standard Version translation of Scripture and occasionally from the New Revised Standard Version. Beyond Scripture, the text primarily references the *Catechism of the Catholic Church* for the convenience of one unified and authoritative reference that is readily available both in print form and online (http://www.scborromeo.org/CCC.htm, which has several convenient search engines including a hot-linked table of contents and index). I recommend reading each chapter and limiting your bible study to the suggested passages on your first pass through in order to grasp most easily the unity and overall themes of each chapter. At a later time, you may pursue further study by consulting the Scripture and *Catechism* footnote references within each chapter. You may also wish see the following references included in this "For Further Study" section, which are sometimes redundant to the footnote references. Finally, you may consult www.GodsPlanforYourLife.org for additional study topics and resources.

Please note that the Scripture and *Catechism* references are not comprehensive but meant to be representative. In some cases, such as concerning marriage and family duties mentioned in Chapter 10, the *Catechism* references are omitted due to the adequacy of the *Catechism*'s index or to the generality of the teaching.

PT I, CHAPTER 1

The exercise in Chapter I considers certain psalms of rejoicing related to being in God's presence and beholding his beauty, goodness, etc. The psalms contain many other instances of rejoicing related to thanksgiving, God's law and to God vindicating and saving individuals from harm, and to God liberating and establishing Israel as a nation. These psalms comprise about half of the total and mainly relate to God's specific work with Israel as a people.

Such psalms of rejoicing over God's care for Israel often seem remote to modern Christians. While Christians are equally reliant on God's provisions, we don't experience God providing our food through the supermarket in the same way Israel did in gathering in their crops. Similarly, we (falsely) believe ourselves self-reliant for our security rather than beholden to God's power. Finally, the very real connection between God establishing Israel as a nation and God making believers in his Son members of his family is little understood.

1. Depictions of God's glorious presence
   a. Moses being in the presence of God: Exodus 34.5, 29-35.
   b. Descent of the glory of God upon the tabernacle: Exodus 40.34-38.
   c. Descent of the glory of the Lord upon Solomon's Temple: I Kings 8.10-13.
2. Those who heed his words and devote themselves to the Kingdom of God are promised to enter into God's joy (Mt 25.21,23: parable of the talents). Those who fail to live for God essentially choose to live apart from him, which is to say apart from joy (Mt 25.30).
3. Other Scripture citations of God plan for us to be with him in joy
   a. For the kingdom of God is not food and drink but *righteousness and peace and joy in the Holy Spirit* (Romans 14:17)
   b. May the God of hope *fill you with all joy and peace* in believing, so that by the power of the Holy Spirit you may abound in hope (Romans 15:13).
   c. Therefore, since we are justified by faith, we have peace with God through our Lord Jesus Christ. Through him we have obtained access to this grace in which we stand, and we *rejoice in our hope of sharing the glory of God . . .* and hope does not disappoint us, because God's love has been poured into our hearts through the Holy Spirit which has been given to us (Romans 5:1-2,5)
4. *Catechism of the Catholic Church* ("CCC") on God as the source of human happiness and joy: 27-30, 1718-2 and on humans' love of the good: 1763-6.

PT I, CHAPTERS 2

In regard to God's holiness, see
1. How Moses shuddered in Exodus 3.1-6
2. How David lost a good man due to carelessness around God's ark in II Samuel 6
3. How the high priest would enter the holy of holies only once per year in Hebrews 9.1-9
4. Disciples goal is perfect holiness II Corinthians 7.1

See the brilliant CCC 599-623 for further reading on Christ's redemptive death in God's plan of salvation. See CCC 651-655 and 658 for the meaning and saving significance of the resurrection. For how we are justified, that is, cleansed from our sins and made to receive the righteousness of God, see CCC 1987-2011, 2017-2026. Other Scripture references related to Chapters 2 and 3 include:
1. Being washed by Christ: I Corinthians 6.11
2. Being baptized into a kind of "salvation loop": dead with Christ, alive with Christ -- Colossians 2.11-16; baptized into his death and resurrection -- Romans 6.3-11
3. Believers' bodies becoming members of the body of Christ and temples of the Holy Spirit: I Corinthians 6.13-20 (and elsewhere)

Another perspective on how we are made holy and given access to God can be found in Paul's notions of being made new creations; see Part II, Chapters 3-8 references below.

Suggested Reading: Raniero Cantalamessa, *The Power of the Cross* (London: Darton Longman and Todd, 1996);

Pt I, Chapter 3

On how Jesus addresses the problem of sin, see the For Further Study section for Chapter 2 in regard to Christ's redemptive death and resurrection and the doctrine of justification.

With regard to "sin" see CCC 1846-76.

The Narrow Gate: What do we know about the necessity of faith in Jesus for coming into God's presence? Its necessary. Can we hope for people who don't explicitly ask for God's mercy in Jesus and believe in him for salvation, but, nonetheless are good people following their consciences as best they can? Complicated question, but, yes, its possible that such people will be given a chance to ask for God's mercy in Christ after they die – but that is a rather risky place to be. Jesus makes very explicit the necessity of his death and that *the many* are headed for destruction, not *the few* (Mt 7.13-14). *Now is the time* to ask for mercy, *now is the time* to share the love of Christ and his saving sacrifice with those around you. See CCC 1257, 1260 and 839-48.

Choosing to Accept Jesus' Invitation: See also the invitation to the wedding feast parable, Matthew 22.1-14.

Leaving Everything to Follow Him:
- Rich young ruler (Lk 18.18-25)
- Hidden treasure (Mt 13.44)
- Pearl of great price (Mt 13.45-6)
- Where your treasure there also you heart (Lk 12.22-23, 31-34)

Pt I, Chapter 4-6

See the following CCC sections:
1. Contemplation
   - Contemplation: 2709-19
   - Praise: 2639-42
   - The Beatific Vision: 2548-2550; 1718-28
   - The Hope of Heaven: 1817-1821
   - Heaven: 1023-29, 1042-50; cf. 326, 328-36
   - Beauty & Glory: 32-3; 341, 2500-02, 2809
2. Intercession: 2629-2636; 2736-7; 2739
3. Thanksgiving Prayer: 2637-2638

4. Role of Scripture in Prayer: 2585-89; 2653-4; 2705-08; 101-141
5. Role of the Holy Spirit in Prayer: 2623; 2652; 2670-72; 2689; 2003; 731; 741; 798-801
6. Prayer in General: Part IV of the *Catechism of the Catholic Church*
    o Section I, Prayer in the Christian Life: 2558-2758
    o Section II, The Lord's Prayer: 2759-2865

Suggested Reading:
- Thomas Dubay, S.M., *Prayer Primer* (San Francisco: Ignatius:2002); see especially section on contemplation on page 83-91.
- Raniero Cantalamessa, *Sober Intoxication* (Cincinnati: St. Anthony Messenger Press, 2005).
- Ralph Martin, *Fulfillment of All Desire* (Steubenville: Emmaus Road Publishing, 2006).
- Peter Kreeft, *Heaven* (San Francisco: Ignatius:1989).
- Romano Guardini, *The Lord* (Washington: Regnery Publishing, 1954).
- Michael Casey, *Sacred Reading: The Ancient Art of Lection Divina* (Ligouri, MO: Ligouri, 1996).
- Thomas Greene, S.J., *Opening to God: A Guide to Prayer* (Southbend: Ave Maria Press, 1977).

PT II, CHAPTER 3-8

To some degree, the material in this chapter spans Part III of the *Catechism*, "Life in Christ", 1691-2558. Some specific CCC passages of note include:
- Holy Spirit as the power to love and to bear fruit, 733-6
    o Because we are dead or at least wounded through sin, the first effect of the gift of love is the forgiveness of our sins. The communion of the Holy Spirit[126] in the Church restores to the baptized the divine likeness lost through sin. 734
- From the Section on Grace and Justification
    o "Holy Spirit is the master of the interior life, sanctifying your whole being" 1995
    o Grace is the help that God gives us to respond to our vocation of becoming his adopted sons, 2021
    o Grace are gifts of the Spirit 2003
        ▪ First and foremost, justifies and sanctifies
        ▪ To associate us with his work, to enable us to collaborate in the salvation of others and in the growth of the Body of Christ
        ▪ Sacramental graces
        ▪ Special graces or charismatic gifts
- Christian Holiness, 2012-6,
- Purpose of spiritual disciplines, 2549
- Man made in the Image of God: 355-61; 1701-15

- Man a New Creation in Christ: 1265-6
  - The Beatitudes depict the countenance of Christ and portray his charity: 1716-7

Scripture passages related to God's plan for our lives (see also references in Chapter 1)
- Matthew 25.34: Place prepared for believers before the foundation of the world
- I Corinthians 2.1: what God has prepared for us
- John 14.3-4: Jesus prepares a place for us

Scripture passages related to God's power at work in us
- John 15.1-5: Apart from me you can do nothing
- II Corinthians 12.9-10: My grace is sufficient for you, my power is made perfect in weakness
- *Phil* 2.13: God is at work in you both to will and to work for his good pleasure
- John 7.37-39: Out of believer's heart shall flow streams of living water
- Gal 2.20: No longer I who live but Christ in me
- II Corinthians 9.13-15: thanksgiving for the surpassing grace of God in the believer
- Eph 1.19: the immeasurable greatness of his power in us who believe, according to the working of his great might
- Eph 3.20 Now to him who by the power at work within us is able to do far more abundantly than all that we ask or think
- I Thess 2.13: the Word of God is at work in believers
- II Thess 1.11: prayer that God may fulfill every good resolve and work of faith by his power
- II Thess 2.16-7: prayer that God may establish in our hearts every good work and word
- Colossians 1.24-29: Paul "rejoices in his sufferings . . . striving with all the energy which he mightily inspires within me" in proclaiming the gospel and discipling believers
- I Corinthians 15.10: Paul's hard work through the grace of God that is with him
- cf. Chapter VI references to how God gives us love for others and doing what is right.

Scripture passages related to believers becoming new creations. Jesus makes us new creations by dying for us (See Romans 6.3-11 and II Corinthians 4.14-16). As new creations, we are filled with God's very own power for holiness and loving others, that is, filled with the Holy Spirit. Hence the saying of Jesus that "his yoke is well-fitting, his burden is light". In this way, we must come to resemble little children. Additionally,
- On the coming of a new heavens and earth: Matthew 19.28; I Corinthians 2.9; II Peter 3.13; Revelation 21.1-2
- God's giving a new heart and new spirit: Ez 18.31; 36.26-27; Ps 51.10-11
- Being born anew: John 3.3; I Peter 1.23
- Jesus makes you a new creation: 2 Corinthians 5.17-19; Rev 21.5; Gal 6.15

Scripture passages related to God transforming us into the image of Christ:
- We (and all creation awaits) our ultimate transformation into the image of Christ: Romans 8.19-23; I Corinthians 15.45-49,51-54; I John 3.2
- Putting on Jesus Christ: Gal 3.27

- Putting on a new nature:; Ephesians 4.20-24; Colossians 3.10-14

PT II, CHAPTER 9-10

CCC passages related to God's power in loving others (cf. the general references to grace above):
- Holy Spirit as the power to love and to bear fruit: 733-6
  - "'God is love' and love is his first gift" (Romans 5.5 & I John 4.8): 733
- The New Law (of grace)
  - Summary of Law and Grace: 1949
  - Grace of the Holy Spirit working through love: 1966, 1971
  - Acting out of love infused by the Holy Spirit . . . strengthened by grace: 1972
  - Love as God loved us, this love is . . . made possible because we have received power from the Holy Spirit: 734
- On the Decalogue and John 15.1-5: Through belief, partaking of the sacraments, and obedience to Jesus, "the Savior himself comes to love, in us, his Father and his brethren, our Father and our brethren. His person becomes, through the Spirit, the living and interior rule of our activity": 2074
- From Grace and Justification Section
  - "Grace is a participation in the life of God ... the Christian ... receives the life of the Spirit who breathes charity into him and who forms the Church": 1997
  - "Sanctifying grace . . . perfects the soul itself to enable it to live with God, to act by his love": 2000
- Evangelism (cf. the US Bishops 1992 pastoral, *Go and Make Disciples*)
  - The Church and the missionary mandate, 849
  - As the Church's right and duty, 848
  - Collaborators in, 927-33
  - Mission of the laity in, 905
  - Missionary paths, 852-56
  - Motive of, 851
  - Origin and purposes of, 850
  - Parents and the evangelization of children, 2225
  - And the sacraments, 1122
  - Source of the desire for, 429
  - And the witness of the baptized, 2044, 2472

Scripture passages related to how God gives us love for others and doing what is right:
- God's pours his love into our hearts thru the Holy Spirit: *Rom* 5.5
- The love of Christ controls us: II Corinthians 5.14
- Corinthians don't just give alms, but *desire* to give alms: II Corinthians 8.10-11
- God put care for the Corinthians into Titus' heart: II Corinthians 8.16
- Paul delights in the law of God in my inmost being: *Rom* 7.22
- Every generous act is from the Father: *James* 1.17

- Cf. Chapter V references to God's power in loving others.

EXAMINATION OF CONSCIENCE (DAILY DEVOTIONAL USE)

The Two Greatest Commandments

I. You shall love the Lord your God with all your heart, with all your mind and with all your soul.
Have I fully embraced God's plan for my life? Have I allowed Jesus to be **Lord** of my life by actively seeking grace to grow in holiness and love? Did I fail to pray daily? Have I lived in **Faith** and trust in God? Am I living in **Hope** of heaven by how I use my resources and time? Do I express my **Love** for God by loving my neighbor?

II. You shall love your neighbor as yourself.
Was I cheerful and caring towards my family and those I have responsibility for? In the chance encounter with a neighbor? Have I **interceded** for those who don't know Christ? Was I humble, kind, generous, chaste, and patient with others?
Have I loved my neighbor through **Corporal Works of Mercy:** feed the hungry, give drink to the thirsty, clothe the naked, visit the imprisoned, shelter the homeless, visit the sick and bury the dead?
Have I loved my neighbor through **Spiritual Works of Mercy:** admonish the sinner, instruct the ignorant, counsel the doubtful, comfort the sorrowful, bear wrongs patiently, forgive all injuries and pray for the living and the dead?
Was I uncharitable in word or deed? Did I give bad example, fight or quarrel? Did I neglect my duties to my husband, wife, children or parents? Was I impatient, angry, envious, unkind, proud, jealous, revengeful, hateful toward others or lazy? Did I gossip or reveal the faults and sins of others? Did I fail to keep secrets that I should have kept? Have I **cooperated** in another's sin
by counsel, command, consent, provocation, praise, concealment, partaking, silence, or defense?

Growth in Holiness and Charity

The Theological Virtues
Faith, Hope and Charity.

The Cardinal Virtues
Prudence, Justice, Temperance and Fortitude.

Gifts of the Holy Spirit (Isaiah 11)
Wisdom, Understanding, Counsel, Might, Knowledge, and Fear of the Lord.

The Fruits of the Holy Spirit (Galatians 5)
Love, joy, peace, patience, kindness, goodness, faithfulness, gentleness and self-control.

The Beatitudes (Matthew 5)
I. Blessed are the poor in spirit;
     for theirs is the Kingdom of Heaven.
2. Blessed are the meek;
     for they shall possess the land.
3. Blessed are they that mourn;
     for they shall be comforted.
4. Blessed are they that hunger and thirst
     for justice; for they shall be filled.

Works of the Flesh (Galatians 5)
Fornication, impurity, licentiousness, idolatry, sorcery, enmity, strife, jealousy, anger, selfishness, dissension, party spirit, envy, drunkenness, carousing, and the like.

The Seven Capital Sins and their opposite Virtues
 1. Pride - Humility.
 2. Avarice - Generosity.
 3. Lust - Chastity.
 4. Anger - Meekness.
 5. Gluttony - Temperance.
 6. Envy - Brotherly Love.
 7. Sloth or Acedia - Diligence.

5. Blessed are the merciful;
     for they shall obtain mercy.
6. Blessed are the pure of heart;
     for they shall see God.
7. Blessed are the peacemakers;
     for they shall be called the children of God.
8. Blessed are they that suffer persecution for the

sake of righteousness' sake;   for theirs is the Kingdom of Heaven.

Sins Against the Holy Spirit
1. Presumption on God's Mercy.
2. Despair.
3. Resisting and/or Attacking the known truth.
4. Envy at another's spiritual good.
5. Obstinacy in sin.
6. Final impenitence.

The Ten Commandments

I. I am the Lord Thy God. Thou shall not have strange gods before Me.
- Did I believe in horoscopes, fortune telling, dreams, good luck charms or reincarnation?
- Did I despair of or presume on God's mercy?

II. Thou shall not take the Name of the Lord thy God in vain.
- Did I blaspheme God or take God's Name in vain, curse or break an oath or vow?
- Did I go to Holy Communion in the state of mortal sin?

III. Remember to keep holy the Lord's Day.
- Did I miss Mass on a Sunday or a Holy Day of Obligation? Was I inattentive at Mass, arrive late or leave early?
- Did I do unnecessary work on Sunday?

IV. Honor thy father and thy mother.
- Did I disobey or disrespect my parents or legitimate superiors? Have I cared for my parents?

V. Thou shall not kill.
- Did I physically injure anyone? Did I abuse drugs or alcohol?
- Have I advised anyone to have an abortion? Did I vote to protect the unborn?

VI. Thou shall not commit adultery.
- Was I faithful to my marriage vows? Have I kept company with another's spouse?

VII. Thou shall not steal.
Did I give a full day's work in return for a full day's pay? Did I give a fair wage to my employee(s)?
Did I fulfill my contracts, give or accept bribes, or pay my bills? Did I steal, cheat, help or encourage others to steal or keep stolen goods? Did I rashly gamble or speculate or deprive my family of the necessities of life? Did I cheat on my taxes?

VIII. Thou shall not bear false witness.
- Did I tell lies deliberately in order to deceive or injure others or to benefit myself?

IX. Thou shall not covet thy neighbor's wife.
Did I dress immodestly? Did I use impure or suggestive words? Did I tell, or listen to, impure stories? Did I willfully entertain impure thoughts and desires? Did I deliberately look at impure television, internet, plays, pictures or movies or read impure material? Did I perform impure acts by myself (masturbation) or with another?

X. Thou shall not covet thy neighbor's goods.
Have I been materialistic? Am I pre-occupied with acquiring things?

Obedience to Church Law: "what [the apostles] bind on earth is bound in heaven", Matthew 16.20

Have I failed to educate myself concerning the teachings of the Church? Did I fail to contribute to the support of the Church? Did I go to Holy Communion without fasting for one hour or more from food and drink (water and medicine are permitted)? Did I practice artificial birth control or was I permanently sterilized (tubal ligation or vasectomy)?

About Parish Life Services

Parish Life Services ("PLS") is a non-profit organization devoted to the New Evangelization and practical faith formation in Catholic parishes. PLS assists parishes in initiating evangelism and practical faith formation (or "discipleship"). PLS also publishes two websites related to evangelization, practical faith formation and parish renewal: www.GodsPlanforYourLife.org and www.ParishLifeServices.org. In addition to working with parishes and groups, all associates of PLS are committed to personally sharing the gospel with those in their midst and helping others grow as disciples.

Parish Life Services is directed by Peter Ziolkowski, who has been active in evangelism and adult faith formation since 1990 in diverse areas ranging from collegiate ministry, directing adult faith formation and hosting a Catholic radio show. Peter currently directs evangelism and small groups at Christ the King parish and has taught a course on Scripture at Sacred Heart Major Seminary in Detroit. Peter lives in Ann Arbor, Michigan with his wife, Theresa, and their five children.

CPSIA information can be obtained
at www.ICGtesting.com
Printed in the USA
FFHW011415080619
52854231-58422FF